A PRACTICAL GUIDE TO
CLIMBERS, HEDGES & SCREENS

A PRACTICAL GUIDE TO
CLIMBERS, HEDGES & SCREENS

‖ ·PARRAGON· ‖

Introduction

Vertical gardening is essential in small gardens where space is at a premium and where privacy is desired. Climbing and scrambling plants of all types can be used. Though flowering climbers, like clematis and honeysuckles, are most frequently grown, morning glory and black-eyed susan, as well as evergreen and variegated ivies and herbaceous plants like golden-leaved hop (*Humulus lupulus* 'Aureus') can also be used to great effect.

A romantic arbour covered with sweetly-scented flowering plants or a secluded corner to escape to for a moment's relaxation is a must for every garden. Though climbers and other screening plants are most often used, fruit trees can make an unusual alternative. Trained against walls or as cordons supported by wires, they play a dual role, both creating a screen and bearing fruits.

There are several types of supporting screen or trellis available and the choice you make is vital to the overall effect of the screen or arbour. It is vital, irrespective of what type of trellis is used, to ensure that it is well secured to a wall or framework as it will be heavy when clothed with foliage and flowers.

Hedges are important in gardens, creating privacy and helping to protect less hardy plants from strong and cold winds. Hedges that are used as boundaries are often clipped to formal, almost fortress-like shapes and sizes, while those that are used within gardens to separate one part from another are more decorative. Small, evergreen hedges can also be used to form intricate patterns around which other plants can be featured.

CLB 4379

This edition published 1995 by Parragon Book Services Ltd
Unit 13-17 Avonbridge Trading Estate, Atlantic Road
Avonmouth, Bristol BS11 9QD.

ISBN 1-85813-807-8

Printed in Hong Kong

Contents

Arches and Pergolas
page 6

Creating an Arbour
page 12

Colourful Screens
page 17

Trellis Tricks
page 22

Making an Entrance
page 26

Disguising Eyesores
page 31

Climbers and Creepers
page 36

Shrubs and Climbers
page 42

Covering Low Walls
page 47

Clematis for All Gardens
page 52

Luscious Honeysuckles
page 58

Wall-trained Fruit Trees
page 63

Versatile Ivies
page 68

Colourful Wigwams
page 74

Hedges to Please Everyone
page 79

Flowering Hedges
page 84

Walls, Fences and other Boundaries
page 88

Index
page 94

Arches and Pergolas

A single arch or a series of inter-connecting structures creates the opportunity to grow climbing and screening plants, forming an attractive architectural feature.

Neil Holmes

Eric Crichton

A rustic pergola (left) made of weathered brick and wood adds height and interest to part of a stone terrace. The dappled light which filters through the climbing honeysuckle makes this an ideal place to sit on a hot sunny day.

The obvious place to grow climbing plants is on a wall or fence, but a free-standing structure offers all kinds of possibilities and creates an interesting focus.

Any garden, whether it is large or small, in the town or country, formal or rustic, old-fashioned or ultra-modern, can be enriched by the addition of an arch or pergola. You may choose to site it in the centre of your garden, straddling a path or incorporated into a patio, or you may prefer to attach it to the house or to a garden wall. It can have the additional purpose of hiding an unsightly feature.

Choosing your pergola
Any construction introduced into a garden should blend with the existing design, as well as harmonizing with the house. Cottage-type houses need the old-world charm of rustic arches and cosy arbours, whereas in the garden of a modern house a pergola might be more in keeping.

Some gardens have a neat, symmetrical design: straight paths and flower beds, for example, with perhaps a patio or terrace created from rectangular paving slabs. This style demands a formal pergola and, to create an even more impressive feature, you could paint it to match the colour scheme in your garden. In an architectural-style garden, it could be painted white or even matt black, depending on the effect you wish to create. Alternatively, to produce a

An arch can be used to bring a feeling of depth and perspective to a garden. This one has a rustic style (above). Smothered in red roses and purple clematis with a strip of verdant lawn running through, it perfectly links the two halves of this cottage-style garden.

ended supports are driven into the ground and the wooden support are fitted into them and then secured with screws.

Where the pergola is free standing and exposed to buffeting wind, however, it is preferable to set the posts in concrete. Dig a hole about 60cm/2ft deep, fill the base with rubble, stand and temporarily secure the post in position and pour concrete mix around it. Be prepared to support the posts with temporary bracing for about a week until the concrete has set firmly.

The first year

Many of the climbers you will want to grow over your arch or pergola may take some time to establish themselves. Even while the long-term plants are growing, though, you can quickly create very pretty effects by using fast-growing annuals.

One really stunning annual climber is *Ipomoea* or morning glory. It is a tender plant, so seeds should be planted in the

Eric Crichton

STYLISH PERGOLA TO SHADE A PATHWAY

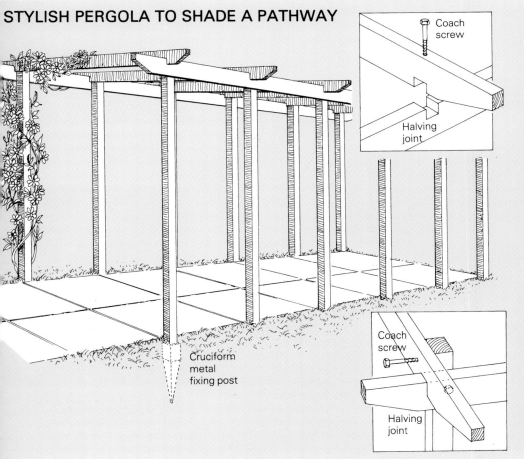

Coach screw

Halving joint

Cruciform metal fixing post

Coach screw

Halving joint

A STYLISH SELECTION

A pergola attached to a house creates an attractive entrance. It can be covered with translucent roofing sheets to form a rain-proof area, or rely on plants to create an overhead canopy of shade during summer. Use a selection of flowering and leafy climbers to create shade and colour.

Bricklaying

Brick pillars, instead of wood, are very attractive but make construction more expensive and time consuming. They can give a formal or informal appearance depending on the types of bricks used. A brick arch connected to the house creates an attractive architectural feature that harmonizes well with a wrought-iron gate. Variegated ivies, such as the Canary Island ivy and the smaller-leaved Hedera helix 'Goldheart', cling tightly to brickwork.

A central focus

A free-standing pergola, straddling a path or paved terrace, creates the opportunity to grow climbers in the centre of a garden. If the pergola is near the house, use climbers such as wisteria and roses, as they will not obscure the view to the bottom of the garden. If the pergola creates a focal point near the bottom of the garden, however, use leafy and rampant climbers such as climbing hydrangea (Hydrangea petiolaris) or the yellow-leaved Humulus lupulus 'Aureus'. Western red cedar creates an attractive shelter with an Oriental feel.

The dark green leaves with gold centres of English ivy (Hedera helix) 'Goldheart' (above) have the great advantage of year-round interest.

The soft, yellowish leaves of Humulus lupulus 'Aureus', (above) the hop vine, brighten up your garden on dull winter days.

Wisteria (above) has glorious, scented, lilac flowers in early summer and makes a stunning display for a pergola.

PLANTS TO DRESS ARCHES AND PERGOLAS

These climbing plants and wall shrubs will produce beautiful flowers and foliage to soften any hard edges and enhancing the overall effect.

mountain clematis *Clematis montana rubens*	Masses of pink flowers in early and midsummer. Some varieties have slightly scented flowers. Very vigorous climber for large pergolas.
large-flowered clematis hybrids	Wide range of varieties, with eye-catching flowers from early to late summer, depending on the variety. Ideal for clothing the uprights of formal pergolas.
winter jasmine *Jasminum nudiflorum*	A very hardy climbing shrub with bright yellow flowers to brighten winter days from winter to spring. Ideal for training on walls and brick arches.
passion flower *Passiflora caerulea*	Tender evergreen with stunning exotic summer flowers and edible fruits. Suitable for pergolas and arches in warm position.
English ivy *Hedera helix* 'Goldheart'	Green leaves brightly splashed with yellow. Ideal for smothering brick arches.
hop vine (golden hop) *Humulus lupulus* 'Aureus'	Herbaceous climber with large, hop-like, soft-yellow leaves from spring to autumn. Forms a dense screen. Ideal for trellises and arches.
climbing hydrangea *Hydrangea petiolaris*	Vigorous climber with dense foliage and greenish-white flowers during midsummer. Ideal for covering large rustic arches. Also grows on walls so that flowers and foliage trail over arbours.
Japanese wisteria *Wisteria floribunda* 'Macrobotrys'	Large clusters of fragrant, lilac-tinged, blue-purple flowers during early and midsummer. White-flowered varieties are also available. Superb on formal pergolas, it is a large plant and so needs plenty of space to grow.

PROJECT   PLANT

1 Dig a hole deep enough to take the entire root ball of the plant comfortably.

3 Tie the stems carefully to the or pergola but not so tightly o will cut into the stems.

The climbing rose 'Madame Grégoire Staechelin' (left) has an abundance of scented, double pink flowers. It grows vigorously and can reach a height of 6m/20ft with a spread of 4m/12ft even in a shady position.

MAKING ROOM FOR ROSES

Rambling roses are ideal for growing over pergolas and arches, as well as trellises. Here are a few beauties from which to make your selection.

'Alberic Barbier' – yellow buds open to creamy white during early summer and often again later in summer. Height: 6m/20ft. Spread 3m/10ft.

'Albertine' – reddish-salmon buds open to coppery-pink from early summer and recurrently throughout summer; strongly scented. Height: 4.5–5.4m/15–18ft.

'Crimson Showers' – bright crimson flowers from early summer until early autumn. Height: 3–3.6m/10–12ft.

'Emily Gray' – rich gold flowers during early summer; scented. Height: 3m/10ft.

'François Juranville' – deep fawn-pink flowers during early summer; sharp apple scent. Height: 4.5–5.4m/15–18ft.

'Veilchenblau' – dark magenta flowers, fading to lilac, during early summer; rich orange scent. Height: 3.6m/12ft.

'Madame Grégoire Staechelin' – pale pink ruffled flowers which darken to carmine appear in large clusters during summer. Height 6m/20ft. Spread 4m/12ft.

BER

Gently loosen the roots to encourage them to spread the plant in the hole.

Water well especially during dry weather, until the plant is well established.

A ROMANTIC ARBOUR

A few rustic poles can turn a quiet corner into a romantic arbour. Use a selection of old-fashioned, heavily scented flowers to create an intimate atmosphere. Honeysuckle, climbing roses, jasmine and sweet peas are ideal choices.

The hybrid honeysuckle *Lonicera × americana* has a strong fragrance, sweet and spicy, and produces an abundance of pretty white flowers. Jasmines are among the most fragrant of all the climbers.

You can create a romantic arbour as a lean-to against a wall or as a free-standing pergola. You will probably want to put a wooden rustic-looking seat in it so that you can sit there to enjoy the scent on summer evenings.

flowering position in spring, only after any danger of frost has past. It then grows very quickly to a height of about 3m/10ft. It has bright blue trumpet-shaped flowers from late spring through to autumn.

Nasturtiums (*Tropaeolum*) can be grown as climbers and their bright gold, orange and red flowers contrast beautifully with morning glory if you grow the two together. *T. speciosum*, flame nasturtium, has scarlet summer flowers. *T. peregrinum* has small, bright yellow flowers from summer until the first frosts. Both grow to around 2m/6ft and seeds should be sown in flowering position in spring.

Sweet peas (*Lathyrus odoratus*) are not only beautiful to look at, they have the additional advantage of fragrance and this can be a particularly delightful effect for an arch or pergola. Most varieties are climbers growing to 3m/10ft, and dead-heading encourages re-flowering.

Unusual annuals

Cobaea scandens, also known as the cup and saucer plant or cathedral bells, grows remarkably fast, reaching up to 3-6m/10-20ft in a hot summer and in a sheltered spot. Its greenish-white and purple flowers appear from midsummer to mid-autumn. 'Alba' is a variety with pale green flowers.

Eccremocarpus scaber, the Chilean glory flower, is another unusual climber, which in very mild areas of the country is an evergreen, but is usually treated as an annual. It needs plenty of watering in dry weather in order to produce its bright orange, tubular flowers.

Thunbergia alata, better known as black-eyed Susan, has mixed cream, orange and dark brown flowers from summer to early autumn. It reaches a height of 3m/10ft in a good summer and seeds should be sown only when all risk of frost has passed in late spring and early summer.

Edible climbers

Another unusual use for a pergola or arch is to use it for a summer crop of runner beans. Before the beans appear from midsummer to autumn, there are attractive scarlet flowers.

Water the plants often in very dry weather and spray the flowers to encourage them to set. The more beans you pick, the more flowers and beans the plants will produce.

Creating an Arbour

An arbour is a lovely, leafy hideaway where you can talk with a friend or sit in peace away from the world, surrounded by wafts of natural scent.

An arbour is a private place, a seat surrounded by foliage that excludes the outside world. Traditionally, they have been used for romantic encounters and political intrigue. In a small, modern garden, the arbour comes into its own as somewhere you can sit and read, have tea, or just enjoy the plants.

The simplest kind of arbour is a small sitting place, enclosed on three sides by trees and shrubs or by trellises covered with plants. It has no top and is open to the sky.

You should aim to create a snug space where no more than four adults can sit. Ar-

A lovely wooden arbour (left) with trelliswork sides, a paved floor and a comfortable wooden bench. A honeysuckle, Lonicera × americana, *covers the roof and* Rosa 'Iceberg' *(seen in detail below) is growing up the trellises.*

Andrew Lawson

Photos Horticultural

David Squire

Japanese wisteria (Wisteria floribunda 'Macrobotrys') will cover pergolas and trellises with its long lilac blooms in early summer (above).

bours are not designed for deckchairs or for sprawling. They are for more decorous sitting, so your four people will not take up much room. An internal area of one to two square metres/yards is enough.

Hedging

The long-term way of making this kind of arbour is to make it part of a hedge. As long as it is a non-prickly hedge it does not matter what it is made of as long as it will prune neatly. Yew is ideal, but very slow, while western red cedar (*Thuja plicata*), another conifer, is much faster growing and responds well to trimming.

Whatever you use should be evergreen (so use oval-leaved privet, not the common one that loses its leaves in winter) and should be rigid in habit.

The evergreen honeysuckle *Lonicera nitida* is useless, as it has to be staked at heights over 1.2m/4ft.

If you cannot wait for hedge plants to grow up, you can use trellis and grow climbers over it. There is nothing to stop you choosing modern materials, but rustic trellis made from larch poles is much better and looks entirely natural when it is covered in plants.

A hedging arbour has a forlorn appearance if you try to make it free-standing. It needs to be part of an internal or boundary hedge, even if it is only a short one. A trellis arbour, however, can be either part of a longer trellis or can stand on its own.

Both types will form a significant vertical feature in the garden, as the height of the

smallest arbour will need to be 2m/6½ft (heads bobbing up and down in an arbour look positively silly).

Clematis and rambling roses are perfect for growing over hedge arbours; honeysuckles and ornamental vines can be allowed to twine and scramble over trellis.

Bowers

Roofed arbours – often called bowers – are more intimate than simple ones and usually have a wide doorway, rather than an entirely open side. They are generally designed for two people sitting side by side or across a corner and, traditionally, their width exceeds their depth.

They were made in several ways, the quickest and easiest of which was to grow trees –

Andrew Lawson

Eric Crichton

usually hornbeam – in a two-thirds circle and fuse them together at the top by bending and grafting when they had grown tall enough. This made a leafy, covered arbour but it was rather large and leaked.

The best roofed arbours for small gardens are made with hedging plants trained on metal frames with hooped tops. The plants take quite a long time to grow and need re-

Wooden trelliswork arbours (above) can be extremely decorative in their own right, especially early in the year before they are clad with climbing plants. The oriental style of this one is emphasized by an eye-shaped patch of gravel in front of it. Fine-stemmed climbers with striking blooms, such as clematis and sweet pea, will complement the delicate design without smothering it.

It is hard to beat the rich colours of clematis flowers (above right). This is Clematis viticella 'Abundance', a late-flowering species which is fully hardy.

This arbour (right), set against a fence, is covered with Russian vine (Polygonum baldschuanicum). This rampant, twining climber very quickly provides thick cover and must be regularly cut back into shape. It flowers in late summer and autumn.

Photos Horticultural

A wooden arbour should be treated with a wood preservative (right) when it is first erected and then given regular coats in subsequent years. Any wooden furniture should be similarly treated to prolong its life. The woodwork will soon become weathered and blend naturally with its surroundings, as can be seen in the picture of a similar arbour on page 908. Siting an arbour against a wall like this provides a solid barrier against the wind.

Trachelospermum jasminoides, which is commonly called star jasmine or Confederate jasmine (below), is a woody-stemmed, evergreen, twining climber that can be grown on trellises, pergolas and even on hedging arbours. It has very fragrant, white flowers in summer, followed by pairs of pods, and the plant is frost hardy.

Andrew Lawson

Photos Horticultural

gular clipping but are delightful. In a formal setting you need only give them 'wings' of hedge on either side.

An open trellis arbour can be provided with a roof. It is best left with a fully open side, as it will appear dank if you try to copy the doorway style. A roofed hedging arbour is a refuge from showers, whereas a trelliswork one is not.

One end of a pergola can be made into an arbour using trelliswork of any kind. Just enclose the last 1m/3ft or so of its length. Pergolas are supposed to be thoroughfares, leading from one place to another, but if yours does not, it can lead to your arbour.

Flooring

Wherever you make your arbour, you should give it a proper floor. Soil and grass will just wear away and cover your shoes alternately with dust and mud. The floor should extend some way out of the arbour, too, to integrate it with the rest of the garden and allow you to sweep leaves out of it more easily.

Simple bricks or small pavers are ideal, laid either conventionally or in a pattern. Large slabs are not always a good idea; they can look out of scale. Keep your flooring free of slippery algae.

Where you construct your arbour is a matter of personal

preference. You may prefer to have it in a corner, or as a niche in the boundary hedge, or even as the centrepiece of the whole garden, opening on to a circle of paving with a fountain in the middle. Some people like to see the whole garden from the arbour; others prefer it to be a completely private hideaway.

Whatever you do, choose a sunny place. Nothing is worse than an arbour that is wet and dark, over which no plants will grow. Neither you nor anyone else will want to sit in it.

Seating

Comfortable seating is important. Stone is not recommended; it looks good but most people stay for five minutes and then move on. Slatted timber garden seating, properly shaped and with a good back is by far the best.

Start, then, with your seating. Decide roughly what size you want your arbour to be, see what seating is on the market, and then design your arbour to fit around it.

The green-painted metal framework of this arbour (right) has almost disappeared beneath a mass of honeysuckle and Artemisia arborescens. This silvery-leaved artemisia from southern Europe can grow to 1.8m/6ft in a sunny site, but it is not reliably hardy and may succumb to harsh winters in cold areas. It goes well with the scented flowers of the taller, climbing honeysuckle because its delicate, feathery foliage is aromatic.

The dividing line between an arbour, a bower and a pavilion or summer-house is a matter of debate. This white, trellised, metalwork structure (below) is a free-standing centrepiece which is attractive on its own but could be readily enhanced by the addition of plants. Climbers could be grown up the pillars and across the roof, and window boxes could be hung from its sides. There are many ready-made designs on the market.

S & O Mathews

Harry Smith

Colourful Screens

Use screens of plants, wood or brickwork to create intimate and sheltered 'outside rooms' in your garden or to hide ugly features.

Screens can play a major part in your garden. They provide shelter from winds or give you privacy in an otherwise exposed or overlooked garden. They can hide eyesores such as ugly dustbins, sheds and unpleasant views. And they can divide your garden into separate areas with different functions.

You can create an effective screen simply by planting a round, mop-headed tree in a strategic position. Generally, though, garden screens combine plants with a wood or brickwork divider.

When planning what sort of screen you need, bear in mind that it should not be allowed to take over. If it is too thick, it will take up too much space and make your garden look smaller. Avoid plants that make dense cover, such as Leyland cypresses, which are fine as hedges but usually too solid as internal screens. Instead, choose trees with thin trunks and upright habits.

A thicket of graceful, silver-trunked birch trees will

A wooden trellis is for many people the preferred method of dividing a garden into sections. It can make a free-standing screen or a 'wall' at the sides of a pergola (above). It provides support for climbing plants and can be painted in a colour that shows them at their best.

Ron Sutherland/Garden Picture Library

provide a light screen of delicate branches and leaves that will always be a pleasure to look at. As well as allowing light through, it will give you privacy and some wind protection. Birches have the added advantage, too, of good autumn colour and their elegant pale trunks make an interesting focal point in the winter.

Space, cost and time will be the deciding factors when you make your choice, and you will need to consider both decorative features and the practical needs of your garden.

A clematis can transform an unsightly wire fence into a colourful screen. Varieties of C. montana are well suited for this purpose, as they are fast-growing and prolific, providing a handsome display of scented pink or white single flowers in spring and early summer. C. montana 'Tetrarose' (below) produces particularly large flowers in soft shades of pink.

Where to place a screen

For the best results site your screen carefully. To work out where you need a screen, move around the garden and sit for a while in different parts of it. Look around you and see where you are most overlooked by neighbouring houses. There may be ugly features that you wish to hide or a chilly wind that makes the garden uncomfortable for you or your plants. As you sit, imagine how different plants would look.

A round-headed tree such as *Sorbus aria* 'Lutescens', planted about 3m/10ft away from you, would make a good screen and your garden would still feel spacious. Sorbus has a round, bushy shape that will blot out an eyesore or give you privacy, besides having the decorative value of an attractive tree. Its greyish-green spring

Don Wildridge

18

Steven Wooster/Garden Picture Library

Trellis work need not be limited to just a single screen; it can be built up into an elegantly formal architectural feature, creating small planting areas as well as a major division between different parts of the garden (left).

A slatted wooden fence can make an excellent alternative to trellis, provided there are gaps between the slats (left). A solid fence would not only block the view into the garden, but also create an area of turbulence on windy days. With gaps to allow a little wind through, however, such a fence can effectively screen off a patio, turning it into a sun trap rather than a wind tunnel.

leaves and white flowers are followed in autumn by berries. As it is deciduous, it loses its leaves in winter, but this may be sufficient if your need is mainly for privacy in warm weather. You won't be using your garden or patio much in winter, so a screen from neighbours is not so necessary then.

All-year cover

If you plant evergreen shrubs or trees as screens, you will have cover all year round. Unless, though, you choose plants with interesting foliage shapes, variegated leaves or attractive flowers and berries, you may be faced with a screen that is sombre and rather bor-

The dense growing habits of the Leyland cypresses (× Cupressocyparis leylandii) – a cross between species from two related genera of cypress – usually make them more suitable as hedges than as screens. However, when there is something you really need to hide, they can be the ideal choice, growing quickly even on poor soils. The hedge here providing a delightful mid-green backdrop to a spring bed (left) is also screening off the compost heap from the rest of the garden.

Michael Shoebridge

P ROJECT A LONG, NARROW GARDEN

If you have a long side wall and a fairly narrow garden, you may wish to add several screens down its length to break it up visually and to create separate areas of interest, such as a play area and a dining area. Use strong trellis sections that are firmly fixed at right-angles to the wall. On either side of the trellis, place purpose-made uniform wooden containers if you want a formal effect. If you prefer a relaxed look, use containers of varying shapes, sizes and materials to anchor the screen. If one area is particularly hot and sunny it would be ideal for a summer display of pelargoniums and annual summer bedding plants. Grow annual climbers such as canary creeper (*Tropaeolum peregrinum*) or plant sweet peas in each of the containers, but remember to keep them well watered.

Andrew Lawson

HEDGE OR SCREEN?

You may find that many of the plants you might use in a hedge are also used to make screens. The difference is in where you plant the hedge, and the role it performs in the garden. Hedges are usually planted along a boundary and offer you privacy, a noise barrier and windbreak. Screens are usually shorter in length and sited within the garden itself. With a hedge you will want all-year, dense cover, but with a screen you may prefer lighter, seasonal cover.

ing to look out on. Aucubas, with their mottled leaves and winter berries, are a good choice for a low, dense screen. Another popular evergreen screen is bamboo *(Arundinaria)*, with its rustling leaves and slender stems. Pyracantha, cotoneaster and barberry all have varieties which are suitable for screens and carry plentiful, brightly coloured autumn berries.

Non-living materials

Screens do not necessarily have to be plants, though they will provide a natural, softer look, if that is most suitable for your garden. Their disadvantages are that they will take time to grow to the required height and size and then they may need pruning. They certainly will need regular watering if grown in containers, and they will need feeding in the growing season.

On the other hand, you may feel a screen made from non-living material such as brick or wood would be the best choice for your garden and these materials can make very attractive screens. The advantages are that they are instantly effective and you can limit their height from the start – no regular pruning needed to keep a brick wall or wooden trellis in trim! One consideration is cost, but this may be balanced against maintenance and permanence.

Ornamental trellis is available in wood of varying rigidity. The most stylish and expensive trellis can stand on its own and doesn't even need to be covered with plants to soften or disguise it, though most ordinary trellis does need supports.

You can make your own effective trellis sections using roofing battens attached to a timber framework. The battens can be arranged in geometric patterns: the effect will be similar to that of ready-made trellis, but it will be much less expensive. Treat all wood for home-made or bought trellis with a preservative that does not harm plants or pollute the soil.

Patio screens

A sheltered patio just outside the house makes an ideal outdoor room for entertaining or just relaxing. For it to work really well, though, you need to create a sense of intimacy. If it is overlooked you may want to give yourself some privacy by creating a sort of dappled shade. You don't need to barricade yourself in with plants or walls to do this: on a patio, a screen of climbing plants grown against a trellis, or a narrow hedge of bamboo, will blur the sight-lines. You will still be able to see out to the rest of your garden, and there will be a good flow of air on the patio, vital to the health of plants grown in containers.

Screens will also offer you a sense of space: as you step out from your screened patio, you will see your garden unfold, and the smallest of gardens will seem to have grown. You can even make movable screens from tall-growing plants in large terracotta pots. Bamboos grow well in containers and will soon provide good cover.

To make a patio screen, insert a section of trellis into an existing built-in brickwork container. Then plant a climbing or rambling rose against

Garages are rarely beautiful objects in themselves, but are often prominently sited in a garden. When they are at the side of the house, their impact can be softened by building an arch of trellis pillars over the drive and covering it with climbers (above left).

If you require a tall screen for privacy – when, for example you have only a low wall separating your garden from the street – quick-growing conifers provide a swift solution. By alternating varieties with different foliage colour (above), an attractive, as well as functional, screen can be created.

Wisteria makes excellent overhead screening. Its woody stems will clamber all over a pergola. As a bonus, Japanese wisteria (W. floribunda 'Macrobotrys') (left) produces pendulous bunches of scented, lilac flowers.

the trellis to provide you with dappled screening. Fragrant plants such as lavender and the tall-growing tobacco plant (*Nicotiana sylvestris*) will provide dense cover at the foot of the rose, as well as fragrance for you to enjoy.

Horizontal screens

Many plants will provide you with horizontal cover if you can give them some supports to grow across. The prettiest is in the form of a wooden pergola. A sunny patio will become a private oasis with shade and hot spots to enjoy. Make an open 'roof' with wooden poles and clothe them with climbing plants. Rambling and climbing roses, honeysuckle, wisteria and even a grape vine are suitable for the horizontal screen.

The resulting cover will protect you from being overlooked and will also filter wind and sun. *Clematis montana* 'Elizabeth', with its rosy-pink flowers, will make a dense cover. If you want perfume, choose the heavily scented, white-flowered *Jasminium officinale*. You can grow different plants for flowering in different seasons, perhaps a wisteria for spring and early summer, followed by a passion flower (*Passiflora caerulea*) for late summer and autumn on a warm patio.

Wind protection

The most effective way to protect you and your plants from a chilling – and potentially damaging – wind is with a screen that allows some air to flow through. A solid barrier against wind, such as a brick wall, can create a certain amount of turbulence or 'eddy' at its top and behind it. This flows forwards, damaging plants in its path. A barrier that cuts down the wind, but still lets air through, such as a piece of trellis or indeed a row of plants, is the best solution.

Windbreak plants are quite tough themselves and are not damaged by exposure. Seaside

FITTING IN

• Make sure your screen, whether it is made from plants or non-living material, fits in with the overall look of your garden.
• If you are using trees to provide a screen, do not plant them too near your house or your neighbour's where their roots could cause problems.
• Choose evergreen plants for all-year cover and deciduous plants for spring and summer privacy.

DON'T FORGET!

gardens have the added problems of salty winds. Use the evergreen shrub *Griselinia littoralis,* the deciduous smoke tree (*Cotinus coggygria*) or *Escallonia* 'Apple Blossom'. All have attractive leaves, and the smoke tree and escallonia offer ornamental value with their summer flowers.

Hiding eyesores

Often the end of the garden is a general dumping ground for bits and pieces that are difficult to throw away. It is often the site of a compost heap and probably the place that most people choose for a shed.

It will improve the look of your garden if you screen any unsightly area from view. Productive screens of soft fruit trees such as black or red currants, a fence of raspberries, or a row of columnar 'Ballerina' apple trees will provide spring and summer cover and fruit in season.

A specimen tree, such as the medium-sized conifer *Chamaecyparis lawsoniana* 'Lanei', if positioned well, will hide an eyesore across the street with golden-yellow foliage which glows warmly throughout the year.

Screens are a way of making a problem into an unexpected, delightful feature, so take another look at your garden and see how you can add a new dimension to it.

Trellis Tricks

Whatever the size of your garden, branch upwards and outwards by introducing trellis – it will enhance its looks and save on space.

A diamond-patterned trellis creates an ideal backdrop for this traditional climbing rose, Rosa 'Galway Bay' (left). The bare wood does not detract from the pretty pink blooms. Because the trellis is attached to wooden battens which are in turn attached to the wall, there is enough room to tie in the roses.

Photos Horticultural

With its diamond, square or rectangular lattice-work design, trellis can perform a number of different functions in the garden. It enables you to branch upwards as well as outwards, training plants to the height you desire. It can be used to mark the boundary of your garden either on its own or on top of a low fence or wall, giving you privacy while allowing light and sunshine to filter through.

Trellis can also be used within the garden as a screen to hide less attractive features such as the compost bin or garden shed, or to give your garden an air of mystery and space by dividing it into separate 'rooms' where a solid screen would have the opposite effect of making it look small and poky. It can also be used against an existing fence, wall or the house itself to support climbing plants or as the framework for a garden feature such as an arbour.

Up and away

Wonderful though trellis is on a grand scale, it really comes into its own when you are trying to make the most of a confined space. By growing just a few well chosen plants upwards and outwards, you can get the maximum display area for the minimum of rootspace.

Trellis comes in a wide variety of forms. Some can be bought as rigid units, while others are sold in a collapsed form ready for expanding and erection in your garden. Plastic-covered mesh types are usually sold from large rolls which are cut to the desired length. Trellis is also available in a wide range of materials.

Made to last

When choosing the type best suited to your garden, you need to consider both its appearance and its durability. It may take several seasons for some climbers to completely smother a trellis while others, including certain roses, may never form a total covering. This type of plant usually looks best against a wooden or painted trellis as this tends to be more attractive than plain metal or plastic.

The main types of trellis fall into distinct categories. Rigid trellis is made either from wood, usually red cedar or softwood, or from plastic-coated steel, and forms square or diamond shapes. This type is readily available from most garden centres and stores. A single piece measures about

Trellis can be used to separate different areas of the garden. Solanum crispum, the Chilean potato tree, scrambles over this trellis (above) bringing it to life with its star-shaped flowers.

Making the most of a confined space, a strip of trellis has been attached diagonally to a wall (below) and a container-grown clematis has been trained up it.

DIAMOND PATTERN TRELLIS

Diamond trellis is not rigid. Attach it to a wall with wooden battens.

SQUARE PATTERN TRELLIS

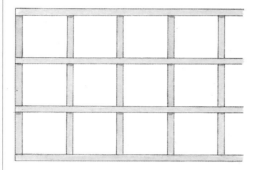

Derek Gould

Square trellis is rigid and can be used as a free-standing structure.

3m × 1.2m/6ft × 4ft, so you will probably need a sizeable roof-rack on your car to get it home, or else have it delivered.

You can also get pieces of rigid trellis in a V-shape. These are ideal for supporting a large-flowered clematis, especially when placed on either side of a doorway.

Wooden trellises are easily fixed to walls using screws and proprietary wall fixings. Rigid, plastic-coated steel trellis is

FAN TRELLIS

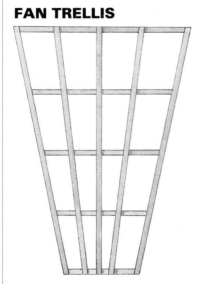

Fan-shaped trellis is ideal for growing climbers in containers.

Fan-shaped trellis can be fixed to a wall as an unusual backdrop for a climber.

PLASTIC COVERED MESH

Neil Holmes

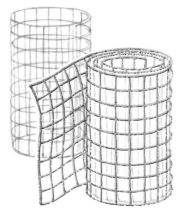

Michael Shoebridge

Garden centres cut lengths of mesh from large rolls.

Grow climbers inside a roll of flexible mesh.

Soften the top of a wall with a climber grown on plastic mesh.

This open structured square trellis (left) is home-made from lengths of wooden slatting and attached to the wall by battens. The charming miniature climbing rose, Rosa 'Pompon de Paris' has been trained into a fan of blooms.

Fan-shaped trellis is ideal for plants which have little foliage near the base but which burst into leaf a little further up. The trellis (below) encourages the Chilean potato-tree to 'fan' outwards following the line of the attractive brick arch.

Four rectangular pieces of rigid square trellis have been fixed together to form a trellis column (below right). Plants have been chosen for their colour and fragrance. Pure white jasmine, Jasminum officinale, complements the honeysuckle Lonicera × Brownii.

David Squire

David Squire

1 Select and mark the position f⟨⟩ your trellis, taking into accoun⟨⟩ plants you wish to grow up it. fixing holes in the trellis.

David Squire

3 Plant your climber 30cm/1ft av⟨⟩ from the wall. Angle the rootb⟨⟩ towards wall. Insert a stake ar⟨⟩ the stem in to the trellis.

sold complete with fixings.

Expandable trellis is available in plastic (green or white), western red cedar or softwood and is easily transported when collapsed. It comes in many sizes, some of which can be fixed alongside or under windows. This type of trellis needs to be secured to wooden battens which are in turn fixed to the wall to keep the trellis rigid. It also needs to be about 18mm/¾in from the wall to allow room for the shoots of twining plants to thread themselves through it.

Roll it out

Plastic-covered mesh is sold from large rolls, which are cut to the length you require. It also needs to be attached to wooden battens on walls. The mesh should be stretched between the battens and secured by turning the ends over and under the batten before screwing both batten and mesh firmly to the wall.

This mesh can also be used

Harry Smith

LIS

Using the trellis as a template, mark drilling holes on the wall. Drill holes in the wall, insert wall plugs screw trellis in position.

David Squire

Eric Crichton

Once the climber is established, it may look a little bare around the base. Overcome this by under-ting with a display of bedding plants.

Harry Smith

WHAT TO GROW

WALL SHRUBS

Many shrubs smother walls with colourful flowers. Even if they eventually become self-supporting, all benefit at first from the support of a trellis, which enables young shoots to be spaced out and trained as you want them.

- Abutilon (*A. megapotamicum*) has a height and spread of 1.2-1.5m/4-5ft and produces yellow and red flowers (Chinese lanterns) from late spring to autumn. It needs a sheltered position.
- Santa Barbara ceanothus (*Ceanothus impressus)* has a height and spread of 1.5-3m/5-10ft but can be kept low by pruning. It is a slightly tender evergreen shrub with deep blue flowers amid small green leaves in mid- to late spring, and it needs a warm position.
- Fremontia or flannel bush (*Fremontodendron californicum*) has a height of 1.8-3.6m/6-12ft and a spread of 1.2-1.5m/4-5ft. Slightly tender, it is a deciduous or semi-evergreen wall shrub that, although relatively large, can be used to clothe a narrow but high and sunny wall. It has cup-shaped, bright yellow flowers from late spring to autumn.
- Winter-flowering jasmine (*Jasminum nudiflorum*) has a height and spread of 1.2-1.8m/4-6ft. A deciduous wall shrub with semi-double yellow flowers from early winter to spring, it is ideal for shady walls.

PERENNIAL CLIMBERS

There are some lovely perennial climbers for trellises on shady walls.
- Clematis species offer a good range of flower colours, but be careful not to choose a variety that is too vigorous. The height and spread average 1.8-6m/6-20ft, depending on the variety. Flowers appear from late spring to autumn. Honeysuckle (*Lonicera periclymenum*) has a height and spread of about 4.5-6m/15-20ft. It has pale yellow flowers with red flushes. Try 'Belgica' for early flowers and 'Serotina' for a spectacular show later in the season.

If your trellis is in a sunny spot, you should choose a climber that likes the sun.
- Jasmine (*Jasminum polyanthum*) has a height and spread of 1.5-2.4m/5-8ft. A slightly tender perennial climber, it has white and pale pink highly scented flowers from spring to early summer.
- Japanese honeysuckle (*Lonicera japonica* 'Aureoreticulata') has a height and spread of 1.8-3m/6-10ft. It has bright green leaves with conspicuous yellow veins.
- Passion flower (*Passiflora caerulea*) has a height and spread of 3.6-6m/12-20ft. Eventually a large climber, it is slightly tender. Restrict it to a trellis around a window. White and blue flowers, are borne from summer to autumn.

ANNUAL CLIMBERS

These are ideal for creating temporary summer colour, with the advantage that you can change the display from year to year. Annuals can easily be grown in large containers on patios with trellis attached to a wall or fence, to provide support.
- Sweet pea (*Lathyrus odoratus*) has a height of 1.2-2.4m/4-8ft. A widely-grown climber, it has many varieties, flowering from summer to autumn.
- Black-eyed Susan (*Thunbergia alata*) grows to 1.2-1.5m/4-5ft high. It is tender and only suitable for growing outdoors in mild areas. Bright yellow flowers with brown centres bloom from summer to autumn.
- Canary creeper (*Tropaeolum peregrinum*) grows to a height of 1.8-3m/6-10ft. It is actually a short-lived perennial, but is invariably grown as an annual. Irregular-shaped yellow flowers are produced from midsummer to autumn.

ROSES

Climbing and rambling roses need support and a wooden trellis is ideal.
- *Pompon de Paris* is a miniature climber with rosy-pink, pompon-like flowers.
- *Rosa ecae* 'Helen Knight' has deep golden flowers.
- 'Étoile de Hollande' has crimson fragrant flowers.

GROWING TIPS

Whatever type of climber you choose, plant it firmly in well-prepared soil, ideally in spring or early summer.

Fork the soil to a depth of about 30cm/12in, adding peat or well-decayed compost. As the soil at the base of a wall tends to dry out rapidly, saturate it a few days before planting the climber. Water the plant a couple of hours before planting.

Put in hole and tease out matted roots from around the sides of the root-ball. Before replacing soil around the roots insert a small bamboo cane to guide the stems up towards the trellis close to the side of the root-ball.

Replace and firm soil around the root-ball, then water the whole area. Later, when the plant is actively growing, lightly fork a general fertilizer into the soil around it.

to form free-standing supports, which are especially effective when used with large-flowered clematis. Cut a 50-60cm/20-24in length of the mesh from a 1.5m/5ft wide roll and form it into a column. Use galvanized wire to secure the ends together, then stand it upright and secure the base to the ground with pegs.

Wooden trellis can also be painted. A green or black trellis will fade into the background while white contrasts with the climber, highlighting foliage and flowers.

Making an Entrance

Create a wonderful first impression by dressing up your doorway with colourful, fragrant and easy-to-grow flowering climbers.

The extravagant effect created by flowering climbers is so easy to achieve and can transform the whole look of your home. You require only the smallest of spaces – and even if the area surrounding your door is concrete you can still enjoy the beauty of a climber as many will grow perfectly well in pots.

Romance in bloom

Whether you choose roses for their old-fashioned, romantic appeal or clematis for a touch of vibrant colour you may be sure of the maximum effect for the minimum effort and outlay. Roses and clematis are among the most popular climbers because they provide both beautiful and trouble-free blooms year after year.

At garden centres, climbing plants are usually grouped together. Each has its own individual label giving the name, cultivation instructions and eventual height.

Splash out on colour

Clematis is a universal favourite and there is an enormous range of colours to choose from – white, pink, red, blue and lavender, vibrant purple or showy yellow blooms. There are hundreds of varieties available and each garden centre has its own selection.

Most popular are the large-flowered hybrids which are a cross between two varieties. They have round, flat, spectacular blooms, which can be up to 25cm/10in across. Generally they have a single layer of petals, but some are semi-double or even double, like a powder puff or a ballerina's skirt.

Hybrids flower from late spring to autumn, according to variety. Some early types have a second, smaller flush of flowers in summer or autumn; while others can keep flower-

Roses add a touch of romance to country houses. This mature climbing rose has aged with the house, draping the porch in a profusion of blossom and rich, dark foliage.

Neil Holmes

ing for months on end.

'Species' clematis are pure bred and less showy, but easier to grow. Their charming flowers are smaller than hybrids, and can be flat or shaped like cups or bells. They are ideal for creating a cottage-garden effect.

A warm welcome

Climbing roses can put on the most stunning displays of all. The single, semi-double or double flowers come in white and every shade of cream, yellow, orange, pink and red.

Some have petals with contrasting edges or undersides, while others change colour as they develop from tight buds to fully open flowers. Many are deliciously fragrant — even more reason to grow them round a front door.

In garden centres, true

Climbing roses can look equally stunning when grown around the front doors of modern houses. This variety (right) – 'Etoile de Hollande' has a profusion of opulent velvety-red blossoms which contrast with the white paintwork to stunning effect. A particularly fragrant rose, it makes an excellent choice to grace a doorway.

This simple porch (below) has been transformed by a mass of large, open-cupped flowers from the wonderful clematis variety 'Nelly Moser'. The fragile, almost translucent, mauve-pink petals are enhanced by a cheeky pink stripe. The long flowering season of this variety ensures any visitors the brightest of welcomes in late spring and early summer.

EWA

Pat Brindley

climbing roses, which have a permanent woody framework, are often mixed in with rambling roses, whose thin, pliable stems are cut to the ground after flowering each year. If you are unsure whether a rose is a climber or rambler be sure to ask an assistant, so you can receive advice on how to prune it correctly.

No two garden centres will have the same choice of climbing roses, but refer to the list on page 94 for climbing roses most likely to be featured. All those listed are 'repeat flowering', which means they bloom over several months, as opposed to 'non-recurrent' types, which flower magnificently but only for a week or two each year.

Buying climbers

For the widest choice, buy in autumn or early spring, when garden centres receive their new stock. Many reputable garden centres will replace plants which do not 'take' so keep the label, just in case! Always examine plants very carefully. Steer clear of old plants that have outgrown their containers. Such specimens may have difficulty settling in.

Choose plants with two or more strong, sturdy stems, at least 60cm/2ft long. Climbing roses should have dormant buds. Roses are sometimes sold bare-rooted, or prepackaged, but these can be tricky and are best avoided if

Insight Picture Library

Pat Brindley

GARDEN NOTES

SOLUTIONS FOR SHADY WALLS

If your front door gets little or no direct sunlight, do not despair! You can still grow some climbing roses, including 'Danse du Feu', 'Mme Alfred Carrière' and 'Golden Showers'.

The extremely vigorous Clematis montana can grow up to 12.5m/40ft tall and has a spread of up to 6m/20ft. It is perfectly possible to use a climber as vigorous as this to frame a front door, but it must be kept in check or it may soon outgrow the whole house. Prudent pruning is therefore essential, to produce an attractive framework. It can be trained to form an elegant arch around the door of a town house (left), where pink-tinged flowers have been chosen to set off the bright red paintwork. The perfection of a pure white clematis (below), grown to form a canopy, adds charm to a suburban house and helps to hide an unsightly drainpipe.

THE BEST CLIMBING ROSES

Roses	Height	Features
R. 'Aloha'	2.4m/8ft	Double, rose-pink, hybrid tea-like fragrant flowers
R. 'Etoile de' Hollande'	3.5m/12ft	Double, deep-red hybrid tea-like very fragrant flowers
R. 'Danse du Feu'	3m/10ft	Double, orange-scarlet, large flowers; no scent
R. 'Golden Showers'	2.1m/7ft	Large, double, golden-yellow, fragrant flowers
R. 'Handel'	3m/10ft	Large, double, cream flowers, edged deep pink, slightly fragrant
R. 'Mermaid'	8m/25ft	Single, primrose-yellow, fragrant, large flowers
R. 'Mme Alfred Carrière'	6m/20ft	Large, double, fragrant, apricot-orange flowers
R. 'Schoolgirl'	3m/10ft	Large, double, fragrant, creamy-white flowers
R. 'Swan Lake'	2.4m/8ft	Double, white, pink-tinged, slightly fragrant flowers
R. 'Zéphirine Drouhin'	3m/10ft	Deep-pink, semi-double, very fragrant flowers

THE BEST CLEMATIS

Clematis	Height	Features
Clematis alpina	2.4m/8ft	Violet-blue, bell-like spring flowers, silky seed heads
Clematis 'Beauty of Worcester'	2.5m/8ft	Deep violet, double flowers in early summer
Clematis 'Ernest Markham'	3m/10ft	Large petunia-red, flowers, late summer, autumn
Clematis 'Jackmanii Superba'	3m/10ft	Dark violet-purple, large flowers in summer, autumn
Clematis 'Lasurstern'	3m/10ft	Deep purple-blue flowers from summer to autumn
Clematis montana	3m/10ft	Bears masses of single, white flowers in spring
Clematis 'Nelly Moser'	3m/10ft	Spring-flowering pale pink petals with carmine stripes
Clematis tangutica	3m/10ft	Yellow, lantern-shaped, blooms in late summer
Clematis 'Ville de Lyon'	3m/10ft	Large, flowers, edged with crimson in late summer
Clematis 'Vyvyan Pennell'	3m/10ft	Violet-blue, double flowers from late spring to autumn

R. 'Handel' is a perpetually flowering variety.

R. 'Golden Showers' does not need a sunny aspect.

C. 'Nelly Moser' with its stunning stripes.

C. 'Jackmanii Superba' has velvet-purple flowers.

PROJECT — TWO CLEMATIS ARE BETTER THAN ONE

Plant clematis in complementary colours. The choice above is the unusual moody blue 'Perle d'Azur' and carmine-red flowered 'Ville de Lyon'. Both flower in mid to later summer.

NO PROBLEM!

Q Why did my neighbour lay paving slabs around the base of his clematis when he planted it?

A Although clematis flower best in sun, their roots prefer cool, damp soil. Placing a concrete slab or large stone over the roots does the trick, and also keeps weeds down.

Q My climbing rose now has two types of shoots, the original, plus new ones with smaller leaves, coming from the base. Should I cut them out or leave them?

A The new shoots are suckers, growing from the rootstock of the variety onto which it was originally grafted. If left to grow, they can overtake the named variety, leaving you with inferior flowers. Dig out the soil around the sucker, tracing it back to where it joins the roots. Pull it off, replace the soil and firm in.

you are not an 'expert'.

Plant as soon after buying as you can, as long as the soil is not frozen or waterlogged. Allow at least 37cm/15in space away from the wall, since soil near a wall is unlikely to get much rain.

Make the hole twice as wide and deep as the pot, and fork over the bottom. Place a thick layer of organic compost in the bottom. Water the plant while still in its pot, then carefully remove it and place the root-ball in the centre of the hole, angling canes towards the wall. The top of the root ball should be level with the surrounding soil.

Return the dug-out soil, mixed with a handful of bone meal, to the hole. If your soil is poor, use rich, loam-based potting compost, such as John Innes No 3, instead. Firm in as you then water.

Giving support

Try to fix the climber to the support before planting, so you don't accidentally damage the plant. You can use flexible, mesh netting for small clematis; stronger, rigid, plastic-coated mesh panels; or, prettiest of all, trellis. These come in collapsible or rigid panels, painted wood or plastic. Battens are thin planks which are attached to the wall first.

Boys Syndication

This rose (above) has been trained to produce a flowering canopy. The delicate peach-coloured flowers pick out the tones of the brickwork.

ween them to provide a cheap and unobtrusive support. Place the first wire 90cm/3ft above the ground and then at 23-30cm/9-12in intervals.

Use soft green twine, raffia or plastic-coated wire ties to tie in newly planted climbers; established climbing roses may need stronger, plastic tree ties. Established clematis cling with their leaf tendrils so they need no help.

Prettily contained

Even if your front door is surrounded by concrete you can still create a lush effect by growing climbers in large flower pots or tubs. Buy clay pots in plain or ornate styles, or for a cool, formal look, use wooden-style Versailles tubs: some come with tall, pyramid-shaped white trellis attached, for instant, free-standing support. To create a cottage garden effect, use old-fashioned beer barrel halves. A large trough can be planted with more than one climber.

The container should be at least 35cm/14in across, so the roots will not dry out in summer or freeze in winter. Put in crocks and fill with a layer of loam-based potting compost.

Fix the supports to these and there will be room for the climbers to weave in and out and for the air to move freely.

Toughened metal vine eyes can be hammered into brick mortar, and galvanized wires stretched horizontally bet-

PERFECT PARTNERS

EWA

The wars of the roses may have been fiercely fought in days gone by but here (above) the red rose of Lancaster and the white rose of York are joined in glorious harmony. Make sure you choose roses which flower at the same time of year for a two-colour contrast. The white rose 'Mme Alfred Carrière' and the scarlet

'Danse du Feu' both flower from summer to autumn. For another stunning combination try growing a rose and a clematis together (below). Here, C. 'Hagley Hybrid' with its pretty lilac-pink, large, flat blooms has been grown with an American pillar rose; they contrast beautifully in colour, texture and shape.

Harry Smith

Disguising Eyesores

Blots on the landscape are inevitable in smaller gardens, but you can make a virtue of necessity and create some spectacular cover-ups.

Robert Estall/Garden Picture Library

Most of us have at least one blemish on our prized gardens – a shed or unsightly wall that our eyes fall on as we plant and prune or, worse, as we sit attempting to enjoy the fruits of our labours.

Such eyesores are inevitable in today's smaller urban gardens, but do not despair, since plants can provide a wealth of wonderful solutions. Indeed, by making a virtue of necessity, the blemish can become the excuse for a glorious display that will inspire a flood of admiring comments.

Unpleasant views
The strategic positioning of a small tree or two can considerably reduce the impact of over-the-fence eyesores. Tree canopies will also screen an unpleasant view from the upstairs windows – the road in front of the house or adjacent commercial sites.

Trees of dense habits, such as conifers, make excellent, solid screens but in small gardens they are often too over-powering and create an unacceptable amount of shade.

Plant instead those with looser habits such as flowering

An old brick wall can be hidden successfully all year round with ivy (Hedera helix). Enliven its dense green leaves with colourful pelargoniums and nasturtiums placed at ground level in containers, or attached to the wall in eye-catching potholders.

31

cherries. The unusually up-right habit of the flowering cherry, *Prunus* 'Amanogawa', is ideal where space is very limited, whilst the autumn cherry, *P. subhirtella* 'Autumnalis' brings welcome floral decoration to the winter months.

When planting a tree to screen something that dominates the garden, consider the place you are most likely to sit and enjoy the view, perhaps a seat or eating-area, and remember that the tree will conceal more if it is closer to you.

Alternative screening can sometimes be provided by a simple pergola, placed above seats or eating-areas and clothed in climbing plants. Wisteria, with its cascading flowers, is one of the loveliest plants to cultivate for this very purpose.

Climbers are the great masters of disguise, offering an abundance of decorative foliage and beautiful flowers for year-round coverage of problem walls and fences.

Walls and fences

Whatever the aspect or area to cover, there are climbers and wall shrubs to suit. Evergreen ivies in a medley of variegations give year-round interest, and can be enlivened in summer with annual scramblers or try a few kaleidoscopic hanging baskets.

Mix climbers of different flowering times to provide colour through the seasons, not forgetting those that have flaming autumn foliage.

The choice is endless, but the classic climbers – the clematis, honeysuckles, jasmine and climbing, rambling or

Gillian Beckett

pillar roses – are magnificent, providing flowers and gorgeous fragrance.

A trellis or a system of horizontal wires attached by vine eyes give the best anchorage for climbers. Self-clinging plants need no support, since they cling by pads on the ends of aerial roots, but these should not be used on damaged or crumbling walls. The less-vigorous climbers are best for chain-link fences which may still need some extra support or an added framework of sturdy trellis.

Always check the eventual height and rate of growth when buying climbers since these vary enormously from plant to plant. Some will take a while to really get going, but quick-growing annuals will provide much plentiful colour in the meantime.

Pipes and guttering

Climbers with soft stems can be tied in around unsightly pipes and guttering. The less-vigorous types of clematis are ideal for this, and the scents of

Eric Crichton

Andrew Lawson

CLASSIC CLIMBERS

Evergreens
Of the self-clinging common ivies (*Hedera helix*): 'Goldheart' – leaves have central yellow splashes; 'Glacier' – silver-grey leaves with narrow white margins; 'Atropurpurea' – leaves purple in winter. *Clematis armandii* 'Apple Blossom' – white flowers flushed pink in spring, needs shelter. *Lonicera japonica* 'Aureoreticulata' – evergreen or semi-evergreen, bright green leaves prominently veined golden-yellow, fragrant white or pale yellow flowers from early summer to mid autumn.

Shade tolerant
Ivies (see Evergreens). *Clematis macropelata* – bell-shaped blue flowers in late spring and early summer. *Hydrangea petiolaris* – self-clinging, very vigorous climber for large walls, large clusters of green-white flowers in summer, will bush out if not regularly trimmed.
Some roses: 'Golden Showers' – fragrant, soft golden-yellow flowers in summer and autumn, best grown as pillar rose; 'New Dawn' – fragrant, very pale pink flowers in summer and autumn.

Autumn foliage
Virginia creeper (*Parthenocissus quinquefolia*). Chinese Virginia creeper (*P. henryana*) – self-clinging, white-and-pink variegated leaves turn brilliant red, prefers some shade. Vines (*Vitis*): crimson glory vine (*V. coignetiae*) – large leaves turning yellow, orange, red and purple; *V.* 'Brant' – yellow and russet with contrasting green veins.

Winter flowers
Clematis cirrhosa balearica – bell-shaped cream flowers, evergreen. Winter jasmine (*Jasminum nudiflorum*) – bright yellow flowers, really a shrub but effective trained against a wall.

Annuals
Some are short-lived or frost-tender perennials best grown as annuals. Sweet peas (*Lathyrus odoratus*). Nasturtiums (*Tropaeolum*): *T. majus* – yellow, orange and red flowers; canary creeper (*T. peregrinum* syn. *T. canariense*) – bright yellow flowers with fringed petals. Cup-and-saucer vine (*Cobaea scandens*) – purple corolla surrounded by green saucer-like calyx.

Neil Holmes

Hide an ugly drainpipe by training honeysuckle (above left) around it. Both it and another classic climber, clematis (above), provide gorgeous fragrance when in bloom. Here, the elegant Clematis 'Miss Bateman' conceals a water butt.

A simple but effective way of concealing a shed or garage is the strategic placing of a plant (left), such as a bamboo, that will not overpower the area.

A well placed hanging basket (right) of mixed blooms artfully hides blemishes ranging from a drainpipe to an unattractive wall.

jasmine or honeysuckle will waft deliciously through nearby open windows. Anchorage can be assisted by trellis boxed around the pipe, or placed on either side with the stems carried across. Make sure, however, that pipes are fixed securely, since established climbers can be very heavy.

Individual pot holders for attaching to rainwater pipes are now available to carry an array of small trailers and bedding plants, though they dry out quickly. Hanging baskets and other wall-mounted containers add further screening colour, and a few large pots around the drain completes the disguise.

However you choose to conceal plumbing, make regular checks to ensure gutters and the tops of vent pipes do not become blocked.

Manhole covers

Containers provide the easiest way of hiding that other unsightly essential – the manhole cover. Group a few pots together on and around it, perhaps placing a trough in front of the most visible edge. (A single container tends to draw attention to the edges of the cover protruding from beneath.) Remember that the pots must not be too heavy to lift off.

If the manhole is near a bed or border, this can be extended around it, with an adjacent prostrate shrub or conifer planted to cast its spreading branches over the cover. In some settings – an oriental-style garden, for example – panels of timber decking make an easily-removed disguise.

Other problems

Dustbins, coal bunkers, and compost heaps can also be major sources of irritation. Because of the need for access,

Photos Horticultural

Gillian Beckett

Turn a disadvantage into a feature by placing a container planted with a bright azalea (above) over a manhole cover. Frame it with dwarf border plants that spill over the cover's edges, or even better, plant them into a specially designed trough that fits in place of the manhole cover.

A well-clipped small hedge (left) is a simple but elegant way to screen off a vegetable plot from the rest of the garden. Should topiary become a hobby, a hedge can be trimmed into a fanciful shape (above right) to solve the perennial problem of screening a water butt.

Photos Horticultural

PERFECT PARTNERS

Brighten up evergreen foliage shrubs or climbers in summer with annual climbers or your favourite clematis. Clematis is particularly good for clambering through tall shrubs, even roses (right).

Mix climbers for interest in different seasons. Plant a vine for autumn colour with a climbing rose, or combine winter jasmine (*Jasminium nudiflorum*) with summer-flowering common jasmine (*J. officinale*). Vigorous *Clematis montana* needs a strong partner such as ivy.

Tania Midgley

these require some form of free-standing screen. Low, pierced walls dressed with climbers, or small hedges are both ideal, but a carefully-selected mix of shrubs gives greater scope for an imaginative, year-round feature.

Evergreens such as acubas, some berberis and the related sacred bamboo (*Nandina domestica*), provide the structure. Add to this some of your favourite herbaceous perennials and, perhaps, a bamboo wigwam for colourful climbers. Plants of erect habit may be underplanted for additional colour in winter and spring.

Climbers and Creepers

A climbing plant can do far more than just scale a wall. It is equally at home trailing from a tub, cascading over a bank or softening the outline of a garden ornament or statue.

Peter McHoy

Climbers are most commonly used to festoon trellises and pergolas with glorious summer flowers, or to embroider walls with leaves that develop rich autumn tints. Yet they can also play other exciting roles in a garden, if you don't think of them simply as 'climbers'.

In the wild, these plants sprawl and scale their way through life, greedily taking advantage of whatever support is available. In the garden, however, climbers are usually provided with a support that both enables them to climb and contains their desire to wander further.

Spreading creepers

When a garden climber is not given support, it will either creep in search of something to climb up or will develop a sprawling and bushy nature. Some climbers, especially ivies, are quite happy to creep along the ground while those with a woody nature usually spread outwards.

Climbers without supports have an unruly nature but they can be trained and used in many different ways, including carpeting an area under a tree, brightening a steep bank or clothing an unsightly tree stump.

Tubs and troughs

When grown in large tubs, climbers are free to trail and cascade, but not to spread or

Cloak a bank in a dense blanket of Persian ivy (above), which will spread on the ground to create a carpet of variegated colour. This Hedera colchica 'Dentata Variegata' has glossy green leaves with golden tinged edges.

Common ivy has been used to frame this statue (above right). Naturally it will creep horizontally and when something crosses its path, it will climb.

talis) at the tub's base, so that the blue or violet-blue flowers of the clematis grow down through the small, green leaves of the cotoneaster.

The orange-peel clematis (*C. orientalis*) should be planted in a large tub and the stems should be allowed to sprawl and cascade into nearby plants. It creates a spectacle of yellow, scented, bell-shaped flowers during late summer and early autumn. *Clematis tangutica* is similar, and also at its best when spreading into other plants.

Japanese honeysuckle

Japanese honeysuckle, *Lonicera japonica* 'Aureoreticulata', is eye-catching in any container, with its variegated green leaves with bright yellow veins and fragrant pale yellow flowers. Unfortunately, this evergreen plant is not suitable for extremely cold gardens.

On a smaller scale, trailing and sprawling annuals are superb for softening the silhouettes of troughs and window boxes. There are many trailing forms of climbing and upright annuals, including nasturtiums, lobelias, and begonias. These can be raised

wander unduly.

Few climbers are more suited to this than Chinese clematis, *C. macropetala*, which normally grows to 3m/10ft when climbing up a trellis. In a tub, where its height is restricted to about 1.2m/4ft, its trailing stems will spread around the base of the container, softening the outline. The nodding, violet-blue, early summer flowers are followed by fluffy seed heads. The variety 'Markham's Pink' (also known as 'Markhamii') is less vigorous and ideal both in smaller tubs and for trailing over low walls.

Terracotta jars

Tall terracotta 'olive' jars are particularly suitable for growing clematis, enabling the plant's stems to trail freely and producing a very attractive display. Because clematis generally likes to have cool roots, position your container with an easterly or westerly aspect rather than one facing directly south.

The types of clematis best suited for containers are those with a cascading nature and a mass of stems. *Clematis alpina* is suitable but can look sparse unless grown with another plant. Try growing fish bone cotoneaster (*C. horizon-*

Honeysuckle may seem an unusual choice for ground cover but it creeps along horizontally just as well as it climbs. Lonicera japonica 'Aureoreticulata' (above) is an evergreen variety.

If you plant a small growing clematis such as macropetala 'Maidwell Hall' (left) in a big stone jar and give it no support it will soon cascade over the side.

With its attractive herringbone shape and year-round display of colour, Cotoneaster horizontalis (left) provides a particularly effective covering for bare walls or banks. In early summer small pink flowers appear, followed by the characteristic rich profusion of bright scarlet berries. In late autumn the glossy dark green leaves turn a warm and glowing red. If you site this climber against a shady, sheltered wall, it can grow up to 2.5m/8ft high.

each year from seeds. If you have troughs on high walls or along the tops of flat-roofed garages or porches, these plants are a must. They will unify your display and hide the containers.

Cloaking walls

Low walls around front gardens can be stark and featureless unless partly covered with a few plants. Flowering shrubs that can be pruned to shape, such as forsythia and bridal wreath (*Spiraea × arguta*), are ideal for softening the outlines of garden gates, but low walls benefit most from cascading and trailing plants. The variegated greater periwinkle, *Vinca major* 'Variegata' (sometimes sold as 'Elegantissima'), has a vigorous sprawling and trailing habit that enables it to clamber over low walls, but for a more dominant yet still cascading nature the deciduous fishbone cotoneaster, *C. horizontalis,* is better. Although not classified as a climber it has a cloaking nature, spreading horizontally or vertically.

Garden steps can be improved in appearance by planting sprawling climbers at their sides. Common ivy (*Hedera helix*) is the easiest form to grow and forms a dense carpet of evergreen leaves and is suitable even if the area is heavily shaded. If your steps are in a sunny spot, however, you have far wider more colourful choices.

Variegated ivies are bright and include the Persian ivy (*Hedera colchica* 'Dentata Variegata'). If you have steps which pass through an arch as they connect two levels of the garden, this ivy will soon clothe the entire feature with green leaves edged creamy-yellow and with white overtones. The Canary island ivy (*Hedera canariensis* 'Gloire de Marengo') is also very attractive, with leaves variegated silvery-grey, creamy-white and green.

Ground cover clematis

Several clematis varieties are ideal for cloaking the ground, especially *Clematis × jouiniana* 'Cote d'Azur', a shrubby

Common ivy, Hedera helix (right), is one of the most useful climbing plants and can easily be grown as either a creeper or a bush. The young runners have aerial roots along the stem and will attach themselves to any surface you give them. When the runner reaches the top and cannot grow upwards any further, it will begin to form a bush with yellow-green flowers and black berries.

Ivies make wonderful ground cover and do an excellent job of filling in gaps and softening the appearance of straight edges. A sunny flower bed with plenty of light provides the perfect spot for the variegated 'Goldheart' (below), one of the many varieties of Hedera helix. Dark green ivies, on the other hand, will grow quite happily in dark areas of the garden.

climber with azure-blue flowers in late summer. Others include *C. tangutica,* one of the prettiest of the yellow-flowered clematis, which has brightly-coloured, lantern-like flowers from mid-summer to early autumn, followed by fluffy silver heads, and *C. flammula* which bears white, fragrant flowers from late summer to autumn.

Highlighting statues

Positioning statues and ornaments in a garden is an art and one that should not be rushed. Large ornaments need to be seen from a distance, whereas small and delicate ones can create a surprise in a small garden, perhaps becoming apparent only after turning a corner.

Small statues can be enhanced by creating sympathetically coloured backgrounds.

Hedera helix 'Buttercup' (above) has light green leaves which turn a beautiful rich yellow in full sunlight. It is resistant to frost and makes an eyecatching splash of colour against a plain wall or among other evergreens.

The Japanese crimson glory vine, Vitis coignetiae (below), is a magnificent ornamental creeper. In the autumn its large green leaves turn all colours from yellow through orange and red to purple and crimson.

BRIGHT IDEAS

CLOAKING TREE STUMPS

Cloak an old tree stump in a climber. Here are a few from which to choose:
- Persian ivy (*Hedera colchica* 'Paddy's Pride') is evergreen with large leaves.
- Canary island ivy (*Hedera canariensis* 'Azorica') is a vigorous evergreen.
- Japanese climbing hydrangea (*Hydrangea petiolaris*) is deciduous.
- *Clematis viticella* is excellent for trunks over 60cm/2ft high.

1-4ft high, then plant a climber to cloak it and turn it into a pretty feature.

Do not plant the climber too close to the stump, as the soil around the trunk will be impoverished and dry. A planting distance of 45-60cm/1½-2ft is about right.

As well as climbers, many roses are superb for smothering tree stumps with summer flowers. 'Aloha', for example, is a modern shrub rose with fragrant, double, rose-pink flowers. It will grow to a maximum height of 1.5-2.1m/5-7ft. 'Juno' is a centifolia type bearing large, blush-pink fragrant flowers, while 'La Ville de Bruxelles' is a damask rose with large, rich pink and very fragrant flowers. Both of these varieties grow to a maximum height of 1.5-1.8m/5-6ft.

Bank and walls

If your garden has a steep bank, you may find it difficult to cultivate. The soil is probably prone to being washed away by summer storms and, even if grassed over, you may find it awkward to mow. A

For instance, bright white statues can be too dominant amidst green plants, but when cloistered with a light-coloured background, and a white-flowered climber tumbling from a wall, they can create an aura of peace and tranquility.

Weathered statues are ideal when positioned against dark green plants such as yew. Alternatively, position them to be highlighted by the sky, with trailing plants around the base to soften the edges and to unify it with the surroundings. Do not use bright, variegated plants, as these detract attention from the statue.

Clothing tree stumps

Digging up an old tree stump is laborious. It is a task, however, that can be avoided. Leave the stump where it is, cutting it down to 30cm-1.2m/

39

Photos Horticultural

Brian Carter/Garden Picture Library

If you're looking for ground cover but perfer the idea of fresh summer blooms to an ivy or vine, then a ground-sprawling rose could fit the bill. The delicate blush-pink flowers of 'Scintillation' (above) bring a fairytale feel to the garden while at the same time solving the problem of that awkward-to-mow area. Rambling and climber roses are not difficult to grow. Several species are so vigorous and thickly-flowering you can use them together with ivy or a vine to grow up the walls of your house.

sprawling or creeping climber could be the answer to your problem. A ground-sprawling rose, for example, will create a breathtaking feature which is also labour saving.

Roses that happily sprawl over banks and walls include 'Félicité et Perpetué' (creamy flowers with a primrose fragrance), *Rosa paulii rosea* (pink with white centres) and 'Scintillation' (blush-pink).

Old, weathered brick walls, perhaps already rich in shades of red and brown, can be further enriched by training a honeysuckle along the top so that the colourful clusters of summer flowers cascade at eye height. Plant the honeysuckle on the sunny side of the wall, preferably where the setting sun can light up the flowers during the evening. Fix supporting wires 10-15cm/4-6in from the top of the wall.

Rambling romance

If you have a rambling and informal garden, with perhaps an old brick shed or garage which has partly fallen down, do not write it off. It can probably be turned into a whimsical and unusual feature when draped with trailers and other plants. Paint the walls white and plant white climbers such as the densely-flowered and extremely vigorous mountain clematis (*C. montana*) to trail and cascade from the top. *Clematis armandii* 'Apple Blosssom' is also spectacular, less densely flowered but with the bonus of attractive leaves. If it is practical, plant your clematis on the opposite side of the wall, so that they appear to cascade over the top. Large areas of white wall tend to dominate the delicately-shaped, blue or violet-blue flowers of *Clematis alpina* 'Frances Rivis', so it is best to plant this variety against a grey background.

Long stretches of wooden fencing, especially when ageing, can be dull and uninteresting. Grow the vigorous climber 'mile-a-minute' vine (*Polygonum baldschuanicum*) to create a cascade of frothy, white flowers from the top of the fence from mid summer to

PERFECT PARTNERS

Dennis Davis/Garden Picture Library

A swathe of clematis falling over a stone wall provides bright summer colour, set off by the Cornus alba 'Spaethii', commonly known as dogwood, planted in the bed at the foot. This attractive shrub with its golden variegated leaves gives support to the clematis in summer. In winter, its brilliant red bark stands out against the grey stone.

Tania Midgley

autumn. It is so vigorous – up to 3.6m/12ft of growth each year – that it can be planted at one end and allowed to scramble right along the length of the wooden fence.

Brightening hedges

Hedges that have become old and perhaps unsightly can be brightened by allowing the mountain clematis (*C. montana*) to sprawl over it. The white flowers, about 5cm/2in across, appear during spring.

Vigorous climbers can also look spectacular when clambering up the trunk and through the branches of a deciduous tree. Choose a climbing rose such as 'Cécil Brunner' with its thimble-sized, shell pink, slightly scented blooms, or 'François Juranville', whose glowing pink flowers are tinted with gold and are gloriously apple-scented. The Japanese glory vine (*Vitis coignetiae*) has large leaves that turn rich shades of orange, red, yellow and purple in autumn.

Honeysuckle (above), or woodbine as it is sometimes known, is one of our best-loved wild plants. In summer it bears pale yellow flowers tinged with purple-red, followed by bright red berries.

Rambling and climbing roses come in all shades and, trained over a pergola or tree (above right), will smother the bare wood in a frothy cascade of sweet-scented flowers to give your garden a delightful touch of old-world charm.

Quick-growing and easy to cultivate, clematis is one of the most popular climbers. A luxuriant fall of the spring-flowering Clematis montana 'Rubens' (right), transforms a featureless strip of plain board fencing into a mass of pale pink stars.

David Squire

Shrubs and Climbers

Many gardeners use shrubs and climbers to build up a permanent framework for their gardens. There is a wonderful variety to choose from and, with careful planting, it is possible to have exciting displays of colour all year round.

Shrubs and climbers form the permanent framework of most planting schemes. They give a garden an established look and add height and variety to the scene.

Every garden has room for climbers as vertical space is generally unlimited. Many climbers have fairly little sideways spread.

They can be used in virtually every part of the garden, but exactly where depends on how they grow.

Self-clinging

Self-clinging climbers are completely self-supporting and can attach themselves firmly to flat surfaces like walls and fences. They are ideal for growing against buildings. Some support themselves by aerial roots from the stems which clamp onto flat surfaces.

Examples are ivies (*Hedera*), the climbing hydrangea (*Hydrangea petiolaris*) and the trumpet vine (*Campsis radicans*). The first two are ideal climbers for shady walls, while the trumpet vine needs a sheltered, sunny position.

Other self-clinging climbers produce sucker pads which 'stick' firmly to flat surfaces. A good example is the Virginia creeper (*Parthenocissus quinquefolia*), which is ideal for shady walls and produces glorious autumn leaf colour. It is a tall, vigorous plant but it can be cut back.

Supporting climbers

Other climbers need additional means of support, such as trelliswork or horizontal gal-

Perdereau-Thomas/Garden Picture Library

The autumnal hues of the Virginia creeper, **Parthenocissus quinquefolia,** *lend a seasoned look to railings (above). All species of this deciduous climber cling easily to walls, fences and trees.*

The curious flowers (right) of this trumpet vine, **Campsis radicans,** *create a clustered look, high off the ground.*

Photos Horticultural

vanized wires attached to walls. Or they can be grown up pergolas, over arches or up tripods of larch poles lashed together at the top.

Colonnades make attractive supports, too. These are simply a line of posts linked with thick sagging ropes. The stems of the climbers may need tying with soft string as they grow.

Styles of support

For these kinds of supports you could use twiners, which twist themselves around their hosts to support themselves. Examples are wisteria, jasmines and honeysuckles.

Climbing and rambler roses are often grown on pergolas, tripods and colonnades but are also suitable for walls. Clematis support themselves by means of twining leaf stalks and they take well to a trellis.

Other climbers suited to any of the above supports are those which produce tendrils. A good example is the ornamental grape vine, *Vitis* 'Brant'.

Another excellent way to grow climbers is over large mature shrubs or up small trees. Here the lighter and less

Gillian Beckett

GROWING TIPS

PLANTING CLIMBERS

Climbers are planted in the same way as shrubs but there is one golden rule that ensures success;
● Do not plant right up against a wall, fence or tree as the soil in this area is liable to remain very dry because the rain is deflected away.
● Instead plant climbers at least 30cm/12in from a wall or fence, and 45cm/ 18in from a tree. Guide the stems to the support with an angled bamboo cane.

vigorous clematis come into their own, like *Clematis viticella* and *C. tangutica*.

Wall shrubs

A wall shrub is one that is grown free-standing against a wall, without any form of support. The wall is generally in a warm, sunny, sheltered position, giving the plant protection from the elements.

Shrubs that are a bit on the tender side are often grown in this way. Examples include

Windows and doorways make perfect settings for the upright growths of Fremontodendron californicum (above left). This tender shrub flowers generously and its shoots, when young, are covered in a soft down. It can reach 2.4-3m/8-10ft with ease and thrives in full sun, needing little pruning.

A more spreading evergreen shrub is Abutilon × suntense (left). It grows to a height of 1.8m/6ft and can spread the same width, making it ideal for the walls of houses, brick walls and even the sides of a garden shed. Its violet and purple flowers bloom in summer and autumn.

Tania Midgley

the evergreen Californian lilacs (*Ceanothus*), *Abutilon × suntense* varieties and *Fremontodendron californicum.*

Some completely hardy shrubs are also grown against walls. The firethorns (*Pyracantha*) species and varieties, for instance, are very useful for shady walls and produce colourful berries in autumn and winter. Firethorns can be trained to any shape and trimmed so that they are quite flat. Remember, though, that the harder they are pruned the less berries they produce.

Also hardy and suited to a shady wall are the ornamental quinces (*Chaenomeles* species and varieties) which carry variously coloured apple-blossom-like flowers throughout late winter and the spring.

Shrubs that retain their leaves all year give a solid look to a planting scheme and contrast well with deciduous shrubs. Do not overdo the evergreens as this can result in a 'heavy' sombre effect, reminiscent of Victorian shrubberies. A good balance is one-third evergreen and the remainder deciduous shrubs.

Care in winter

Some evergreens are on the tender side and will not survive hard winters. Examples include shrubby veronicas (hebes), which have a very long flowering season in summer, and the summer-flowering escallonias and sun roses (*Cistus*).

For hard-winter areas choose tough evergreens like *Elaeagnus pungens* 'Maculata', with its gold-splashed leaves that show up well in winter. Berberis, such as *B. darwinii* and *B. × stenophylla,* both spring flowering, will produce magnificent displays, of deep yellow blooms.

Deciduous shrubs

These create a lighter, more airy effect in planting schemes and the great advantage is that they reflect the seasons. This is quite dramatic in some: the golden-yellow spring blossom of forsythia, for example, the fiery autumn leaf colour of the smoke bush (*Cotinus coggygria*) or the spidery yellow flowers of witch hazel (*Hamamelis × intermedia*) in the depths of winter.

Flowering shrubs

Shrubs that produce an attractive flower display are undoubtedly the most popular. If space permits, plant shrubs for each season of the year.

Try also to choose shrubs that flower for a long period, as they are worth the space they take up. Some popular shrubs, however, have but a fleeting display. Forsythia, which heralds the spring everywhere, is one such.

The charming white and pink-splashed flowers of Clematis chrysocoma *(right) will flower in midsummer and often into autumn. Like all* Clematis *creepers, it will cling naturally on twining stalks. Here, it blends with the spreading dwarf shrub,* Chaenomeles speciosa *'Phylis Moore'.*

For those who like a hardy, woodland creeper, a fine choice is Camellia × williamsii' *'Donation' (far right). Its showy, cup-shaped flowers appear mainly in spring.*

With a delightful scent, like lily-of-the-valley, the evergreen Mahonia japonica trifurca *(below right) makes a dependable choice for winter shrubbery. Lemon flowers appear in winter.*

*Subtler colours, to offset brighter plants, are found (below) on a smoke tree (*Cotinus coggygria *'Foliis Purpureis'), with its purple midsummer leaves.*

In spring the varieties of *Camellia × williamsii* flower over a long period but need lime-free (acid) soil. The dwarf ground cover shrub *Erica × darleyensis* (a heather) flowers in winter and spring and it has many varieties. Unlike most heathers it grows in limy soil.

For summer there are several long-flowering shrubs, especially the shrubby cinquefoils (*Potentilla*) that have masses of single rose-like flowers. The ground-covering lings (*Calluna vulgaris* varieties) flower for a long period in summer and are ideal for planting around larger shrubs, but must have lime-free soil.

Hardy fuchsias bloom from mid-summer until autumn as do many shrubby veronicas (hebes). Modern repeat-flowering shrub roses are essential in the mixed border.

Autumn-flowering shrubs include *Caryopteris × clandonensis* and varieties, a dwarf shrub popularly called blue spiraea. There are numerous shrubs with autumn berries, such as cotoneasters, spindle (*Euonymus europaeus* 'Red Cascade' is a good one) and deciduous berberis hybrids, all with a long display.

Eric Crichton

S & O Mathews

Tania Midgley

Peter McHoy

Winter-flowering shrubs well worth growing are *Mahonia japonica* with fragrant yellow flowers, and the white-flowered laurustinus (*Viburnum tinus*), both of which are evergreen.

Foliage shrubs

Shrubs noted for their attractive foliage are gradually becoming more popular. They are highly recommended as they have a long period of interest. This is true even of the deciduous kinds.

Some deciduous shrubs provide glorious autumn leaf colour. Good examples of this are smoke bush (*Cotinus coggygria* and varieties), Japanese maple (*Acer palmatum* varieties) and red chokeberry (*Aronia arbutifolia*).

SEMI-EVERGREENS

Semi-evergreen shrubs and climbers are those that drop some or all of their leaves during a hard winter, but retain them when winters are mild, or when grown in mild areas.

Examples include the shrubs *Cotoneaster* 'Cornubia'; *Cotoneaster simonsii; Lonicera fragrantissima* and other winter-flowering shrubby honeysuckles; *Lonicera pileata;* the oval-leaved privet (*Ligustrum ovalifolium*) which is often used for hedging; *Rhododendron mucronatum;* and winter-flowering *R.* 'Praecox'.

Semi-evergreen climbers include the honeysuckle *Lonicera japonica* and its well-known and popular variety 'Aureoreticulata' that has conspicuously gold-veined leaves.

Snow-covered blooms (above) display Cotoneaster × watereri 'Cornubia' at its winter best. Shrubs grow on patios, too. This hydrangea in a terracotta pot (below) has a healthy balance of warmth and light.

There are deciduous coloured-leaved shrubs which provide a far longer display than any flowering shrub. They include the golden mock orange (*Philadelphus coronarius* 'Aureus') and the purple smoke bush (*Cotinus coggygria* 'Foliis Purpureis' and 'Royal Purple'). There are variegated shrubs, too, like the shrubby dogwood (*Cornus alba* 'Elegantissima') with its white and green foliage.

All of these go well with flowering shrubs and blend well with other plants such as herbaceous perennials.

Using shrubs

Here are more ideas to help you make the most of your shrubs in the garden.

In shrub and mixed borders plant the tallest shrubs at the back, those of medium height in the middle and dwarf shrubs at the front. Mix deciduous and evergreen as much as possible. Spread shrubs for different seasons evenly through the border and position scented ones at the front.

A good way of combining shrubs and other plants in a mixed border is to create little groups with seasonal interest. For summer colour you could plant perennials like irises and foxgloves with deutzias

(flowering shrubs) and a purple-leaved smoke bush.

An autumn and winter scheme could consist of *Mahonia japonica* with the red-stemmed dogwood (*Cornus alba* 'Sibirica') and lenten rose (*Helleborus orientalis*) interplanted with snowdrops.

For spring try a forsythia underplanted with blue grape hyacinths (*Muscari.*) Grow a *Clematis viticella* through the forsythia to produce colour in summer when the forsythia has ceased flowering.

Specimen planting is possible with shrubs that have a distinctive form of growth. They can be grown singly in lawns or other parts of the garden to act as focal points.

Examples are the yuccas with their stiff, erect, sword-shaped leaves; *Fatsia japonica* with its large, evergreen, hand-shaped leaves; the mushroom-shaped purple-leaved Japanese maple (*Acer palmatum* 'Dissectum Atropurpureum'); the corkscrew hazel (*Corylus avellana* 'Contorta') with its curly shoots; and stag's horn sumach (*Rhus typhina*) which has large palm-like leaves noted for brilliant autumn colour.

Container growing is possible if you choose the right shrubs and plant them in tubs at least 30cm/12in in diameter and depth.

Again, yuccas, fatsia and Japanese maples are suitable, together with rhododendrons, camellias (lime-free compost for both), hydrangeas, the golden-leaved evergreen *Choisya ternata* 'Sundance', heathers, the evergreen *Euonymus fortunei* varieties and hollies, especially those grown formally and clipped.

Flower-arranging enthusiasts will find many shrubs a delight. The gold-streaked leaves of *Eleaegnus pungens* 'Maculata' are arresting in winter, as can be the rich purple and green foliage of *Pittosporum tenuifolium*, one of the hardiest shrubs.

Photos Horticultural

Gary Rodgers/Garden Picture Library

Covering Low Walls

There are many things you can do to alter the appearance of a low garden wall. You can decorate it, disguise it, or enhance it with some well-chosen plants.

A low wall in a garden can sometimes be a really attractive feature. Even if a wall is not that attractive, much can be done to enhance it.

If you are fortunate enough to have a well-built dry-stone wall, you could tuck some colourful plants into the crevices. The mellow tones of a brick wall provide the perfect backdrop for greenery and flowers, and walls made of preformed concrete blocks have decorative holes through which climbing plants can twine.

Wall containers

Whatever material it is made of, any low wall can be brightened up with containers. Wire baskets with flat sides are made specially for fixing to walls. Pretty terracotta containers, also with flat backs and with fixing holes drilled through them, are available in many different shapes. Plant them with cascades of lilac, pink, purple or red aubrieta, blue or white *Campanula carpatica,* blue lobelia, pink or white arabis, and yellow *Alyssum saxatile.* Universal pansies and trailing ivies are pretty for cheerless winter months. Line the baskets with black polythene or spaghnum moss and when filling containers place pieces of broken clay pots in the bottom before filling them with compost.

To liven up the top edge of a wall, you can place planting boxes on it. They should be lifted a little above the wall to allow for drainage, perhaps on tiles or bricks. If there is any danger that they might fall off or be blown over, it would be wise to secure them in some way to the wall.

Planting boxes

Boxes can contain whatever you prefer, but try to give them height here and there. Use dwarf conifers of differing shapes and colours. Trailing plants create interesting shapes and colour when draped against bricks.

You can change the contents of your boxes seasonally. A good way to do this is to plant up several plastic box liners in advance which you can then change as plants pass their best. A liner of blooming bulbs can be moved out to die back and multiply out of sight to be

Ron Sutherland/Garden Picture Library

Greenery and flowers spill out of this dry-stone wall. The open structure of these walls, full of gaps and spaces, makes for particularly easy planting.

47

Peter McHoy

GROWING TIPS

RAIN SHADOW

When planting climbers close to walls, do not position them so that they are within the rain shadow. This is the area of soil that is normally sheltered from rain by the wall. The roots of plants growing within this area are unlikely to get sufficient water to survive.

replaced by one planted with, say, summery impatiens (busy Lizzie), marigolds or petunias.

Tomato plants can create an unusual summer display as well as provide tasty morsels for your table. The 'Tumbler' variety, now obtainable at garden centres, hangs loosely and produces profuse fruit if regularly fed and watered. For winter colour, try a collection of winter-flowering heathers. Heathers nearly all dislike lime so you can keep one liner full of ericaceous compost to accommodate them.

A touch of terracotta

Terracotta troughs can look marvellous on top of old brick walls. You can buy 'feet' for these to lift them for drainage. Dwarf rhododendrons look lovely in them, planted with ivy or variously coloured aubrieta hanging over and down the wall. Remember that rhododendrons, like heathers, require ericaceous compost to survive. A terracotta trough is ideal as a temporary home for houseplants that provide bright colour during the summer but are too tender to remain outdoors all year round.

Another way to add life to a low wall is to construct a little rockery along the top of it. You can use builders' rubble for

this. A builders' yard can provide this, or you may have enough discarded builders' debris in your own garden already. Choose enough nicely shaped and rounded pieces to cover the top of your wall and cement them in place, leaving little pockets for the plants and cracks for drainage.

Fill the pockets with compost and plant rock plants such as helianthemum (rock

In this romantic garden (below), a low wall has been used to divide the lawn. Notice the delicate combination of colours: cotoneaster tumbles over the wall top and side, silver-leaved senecio and purple lavender surround the base of the wall.

rose) which comes in a wide range of colours, *Dianthus alpinus,* mossy saxifrage, *Sedum acre* (stonecrop) and perhaps some crocus, which do not need deep planting, for spring colour. Then keep the plants nicely moist until they are established. Remember that you cannot grow lime-hating plants near cement or mortar as the lime content is too high for them.

Clever disguise

If you find your wall so ugly that you want to disguise it completely, you can cover it with a creeping foliage plant. *Parthenocissus henryana,* for

Ron Sutherland/Garden Picture Library

Peter McHoy

instance, often mistaken for Virginia creeper, will quickly cover a wall with white, pink and green leaves which turn a pretty red in autumn. Its tendrils cling well to the wall's rough texture but it may need a little support with a cane at first. Foliage completely covering a wall will also make a stunning backdrop for containers of colourful flowers.

Holes in ornamental concrete block walls are perfect for the tendrils of strong climbers, such as honeysuckle, which do not cling but wind around themselves. Choose a colourful and scented climber, like *Lonicera × americana*.

Honeysuckle is deciduous, however. If you want leaf cover all year, try ivy instead, but not just any ivy. There are delightful, small-leaved variegated types such as *Hedera helix* 'Manda's Crested' which goes reddish in winter or *H.h.* 'Jubilee' which has red stems; 'Goldheart' is a similar leafy variety.

Mossy growth

If your wall is in the right position – often damp or facing away from the sun – you can encourage moss to grow on it. This is quite easily done by painting areas of the wall with a mixture of yoghurt or sour milk and liquid fertilizer. As this tends to smell a little unpleasant, you might prefer just to spray it with fertilizer instead. In either case, keep the wall wet until the moss starts

This low wall (above) has been faced with artificial stone, and gaps left here and there for planting. Greys, greens and accents of orange and dark red complement and contrast with the colour of the wall, and the whole is offset against a backdrop of dark conifers.

A decorative pierced brick wall (above right) provides solid support for a pink climbing rose.

A magnificent display of brightly coloured geraniums (pelargonium) has transformed the appearance of this drab stone wall (right).

Photos Horticultural

DISGUISING WALLS

You can change the look of an unsightly low brick wall by covering it with a veneer of brick or stonework. These flat slabs, available from large garden centres or DIY centres, are mortared onto the original wall. Make sure the slabs are for external use. For a good finish, dig down to the foundation.

BRIGHT IDEAS

Eric Crichton

Plants that are suitable for rockeries will have no trouble finding a root-hold in the most difficult nooks and crannies. Here (left), a bold splash of Dianthus and thrift brighten grey stonework.

A delightful clump of viola (right) has happily established itself in the narrow gaps between these stones, while Campanula portenschlagiana (below) spreads along the base of this wall, thriving where other plants would fail.

David Squire

to form. This will be easier under any containers fixed to the wall as these have to be regularly watered.

You probably will not want to make holes deliberately in pretty new walls in order to accommodate plants. Old walls, if they do not already have cracks in them, are another matter altogether.

A little gentle chiselling can widen a gap into which compost can be pushed and a plant inserted. In a very dry season you may need to pay some attention to watering until the roots have taken but, brick being porous, most plants will survive the usual fluctuations in temperature and rainfall in summer. Wallflowers, so named because they grow out of walls, are perfect. The prettiest for this job are the small, 15cm/6in Tom Thumb Series in reds or oranges.

Filling the gaps

Gaps at the top of old walls can be filled with the hardy, evergreen hummocks of armeria (thrift) which in summer has fluffy pink flowers. Consider sempervivium (houseleek), which actually enjoys living in dry walls.

There are many other plants which are suitable for growing in walls. Choose from sedum, saxifrage, campanula and *Lewisia cotyledon howellii*, which flowers apricot-pink in summer, and is specially adapted for vertical planting.

Although you might want to increase the height of your low wall, it is not always possible to find matching bricks or concrete blocks. Additionally, if the wall is a boundary wall, making it higher could upset

Eric Crichton

SUGGESTED CLIMBERS AND WALL SHRUBS

● Clematis flowers in spring or summer. The flowers love sun, but roots need shading.
● Hop-vine (*Humulus lupulus*)
This fast growing climber has clusters of yellowish-green flowers.
● Passion flower (*Passiflora caerulea*)
This vigorous climber is smothered with 7.5cm/3in flowers through summer.
● Russian vine (*Polygonum baldschuanicum*)
This very fast-growing deciduous climber produces white flowers in summer.
● Japonica/Japanese quince (*Chaenomeles speciosa*)
The red flowers in early spring turn into golden fruit.
● Euonymus (*Euonymus fortunei*)
This trailing evergreen will tolerate shade.
● *Garrya elliptica*
This quick-growing shrub has grey-white catkins in mid-winter.
● Hydrangea (*Hydrangea petiolaris*)
A self-clinging climber, covered in white flowers in early to midsummer.

For those who want to grow something really different on their walls, Sempervivum 'Gamma' (right) is an excellent choice. These succulents are normally seen in rock gardens, but are equally happy in the well-drained soil of dry walls.

Collections/Patrick John

A colourful row of polyanthus (below) does wonders in cheering up this terrace with its low dividing wall. Velvety moss has been allowed to spread over the side of the wall to soften the dark stone.

even the friendliest of neighbours. But using your already sited low wall as a strong support for a tough trellis will cause suspicion only until the profusion of climbing plants you choose starts to decorate your neighbours' side with a living mantle of colour.

This type of trellis must be very strong to resist winds and should be firmly fixed to the wall. If this is difficult, the trellis supports could be inserted into special heavy spiked metal post holders. These hold the posts just above the ground so that they do not rot. Drive in posts about 10cm/4in away from the wall to avoid the base. DIY stores and many garden centres can provide trellis and posts. The strongest trellis is the type made with square slats. They are normally already treated with wood preservative but if you want to apply an extra coat, only use one that is not harmful to plants.

Cloaked in greenery

There are many climbers you can grow through a trellis, but varieties of *Clematis montana*, such as 'Elizabeth', which has masses of shell-pink scented flowers in spring, is among the prettiest. It will shoot up very quickly. The wine-red stems and leaves will wind in and out of the openings in the trellis (and of ornamental block)

and will just need tidying. Prune it only after it has flowered. Nothing the amateur pruner can do would harm this clematis. Plant the clematis – as you should all climbers, near walls – about 30cm/1ft away from the base.

Private pergola

Another way of creating some privacy from a low wall without upsetting the neighbours, is to build a pergola against it – the kind everybody has seen in Mediterranean countries, usually festooned with grapes. You could lay a patio beneath for sunbathing or barbeques.

Choose the sunniest part of the wall and plan out a patio, perhaps leaving spaces between the stones for herbs (thyme smells marvellous if you step on it) and little perennials such as pinks. Then site the pergola against as much of the wall as you feel like using. Any good DIY store will advise on construction, or find a local builder or carpenter to build it for you .

There are many climbing plants that will happily ramble across your pergola, including hardy vines which will dangle bunches of grapes. For a rose-covered arbour, try the fragrant yellow climbing rose, 'Golden Showers'.

For winter, the scented yellow *Jasminium nudiflorum*, is a trouble-free choice.

Clematis for All Gardens

The clematis genus contains many of the very best climbing plants, producing attractive flowers in an enormous variety of shapes and colours.

If ever a plant deserved the title 'Queen of Climbers', clematis does. This handsome genus of plants offers literally hundreds of gorgeous varieties. The choice of flower colour ranges from subtle, pastel shades of pink, blue and mauve, to the more regal hues of crimson, magenta and purple. Rich creams are available, as are stunning whites and vibrant yellows.

Some varieties produce an abundance of small, delicate, single or double blooms, while others have fewer, but more imposing flowers. Some have seed heads so beautiful that they are much sought after for flower arrangements.

Clever clematis

The clematis family can supply a glorious climber suitable for virtually any site. Exposed, chilly, north-facing walls are absolutely no problem to *C. alpina* or *C. macropetala* varieties, for example, while an ugly shed, wall or outbuilding can soon be camouflaged by any member of the vigorous *C. montana* branch of the family.

Clematis will clothe and soften the outlines of arches and pergolas with enchanting displays of flowers. By selecting your varieties carefully, you can have blooms from spring to autumn.

Trees and shrubs whose interest is limited to early spring need not be an embarrassment for the rest of the season. You can grow a clematis through them. Varieties of *C. jackman-*

The early summer blooms of 'Nelly Moser' are best in semi-shade; the carmine stripe fades in full sun.

Eric Crichton

52

PLANT PROFILE

Suitable site and soil Likes a deep, moist, cool root run. Will thrive in almost any good quality garden soil. Sandy or chalky soils must have plenty of organic matter added to help retain moisture. Do not plant too near to thirsty hedges (especially privet) or trees as these will rob the clematis of moisture. Clematis appreciates a bit of lime, but it is not essential.

Planting Container grown clematis may be planted at any time as long as the soil retains some warmth. Early autumn or late spring are best.

Cultivation and care When, where and how to prune depends on the variety; read the instructions carefully when you buy.

Clematis must be fed regularly with a liquid fertilizer in the growing season. In autumn, mulch with farmyard manure or work in bone meal around the stem.

Propagation Cuttings are best left to the professional. Layering in summer is an easier method. Fill a 10-15cm/4-6in flowerpot with cutting compost and sink into the ground a little away from the parent so you do not damage roots. Bend a young shoot until it touches the soil in the pot. Make a slit upwards from below a leaf node, and dust it with hormone rooting powder. Cover with soil and clip into place with a bent piece of wire. Cover with a stone or slate to keep pot moist and cool. Keep pot damp. Sever the young plant from the parent the following spring and plant in the usual way.

Pests and diseases Clematis wilt tends to attack young plants. Remove and destroy infected stems immediately. With luck new stems will form. Spraying the leaves and soaking the immediate root area with a benomyl fungicide will help to protect new growth. If you lose your plant, replace the surface soil at the site and grow a different variety. If the trouble persists, plant a species clematis in new soil, as they are less susceptible than cultivated varieties.

Mildew may be a problem, especially to some hybrids. Spray with a proprietary fungicide.

Photos Horticultural

ii and *C. viticelli* are useful for this. *C. montana* is a particularly handy choice if you wish to cover a large tree or to disguise a dead one.

Clematis can be used as ground cover. Once again *C. montana* may be called into service. Other suitable subjects are varieties of *C. alpina*, *C. macropetala*, *C. orientalis* and *C. tangutica*. Any of these plants also look lovely if allowed to tumble down a bank.

There are even a few herba-

ceous species suitable for the mixed border, including *C. integrifolia* and *C. recta*.

Flowering types

There are so many species and varieties of clematis that it is useful to split them into three groups, depending on the season when they flower, their growing habit and their pruning requirements.

The first group includes the *Clematis montana* varieties, along with *C. macropetala* and

Harry Smith Collection

There is great variety in the shapes, as well as the colours, of clematis flowers. The late flowering, pendulous, golden yellow blooms of C. tangutica (above) have a lantern shape, while the summer flowers of the herbaceous, late-flowering C. integrifolia (left) are deep blue bells. These are succeeded later in the year by very attractive, light-brown seed heads. The most readily recognizable of all clematis flower forms, though, are the abundant, flat, single blooms of C. montana (right) which appear in late spring.

Eric Cricnton

C. alpina. All are vigorous, fully hardy, and produce masses of blooms in late spring. Pruning should be restricted to merely tidying up the plant. Dead flower heads and stems should be removed immediately after flowering so the new growth ripens before winter.

C. montana 'Elizabeth' can reach a height of 10-12m/30-40ft and bears soft pink, scented flowers, while *C. m.* 'Tetrarose' is a stronger, satin pink variety that reaches a height of 7-8m/23-26ft.

Macropetala and alpina varieties are good looking and very hardy. *C. macropetala* 'Markham's Pink' has delicate, bell-shaped flowers in a glorious dusky pink. It grows to a height of 3m/10ft and blooms appear in late spring and summer. It is a suitable clematis for a small garden.

C. alpina 'Frances Rivis' is a lovely bell-shaped variety in a mid-blue colour. 'Ruby' has purplish-pink blooms. They are free flowering in spring with an occasional second flush in summer. The delicate, fluffy, silver seed heads are produced in the summer

months. These varieties also suit small gardens, reaching a height of 2-3m/6-10ft.

Early flowers

The second group includes early flowering, frost hardy subjects. These should be pruned back to the lowest pair of strong buds in their first season, so that growth is more vigorous. In subsequent seasons, pruning should be restricted to removing dead growth only, because the flowers are only produced on the previous year's stems.

'Nelly Moser' is an old favourite in this group. It produces large, single, flat rose coloured flowers that have a carmine stripe on each petal. Blooms appear in early summer on plants that reach a height of 3.5m/11ft. The flower colours fade in strong sunlight so it is best to plant these in a shaded east, west or north facing site.

'Proteus' has wide, double mauve-pink flowers. This handsome variety produces blooms in early summer and a second flush of single flowers later in the season. It reaches

RECOMMENDED VARIETIES

'Crimson King'. Height 2.4-3m/8-10ft. Has large, striking, clear crimson flowers in summer and autumn.

C. alpina 'Willy'. Height 2-3m/6-10ft. Has delicate white, lantern-shaped flowers in abundance in spring. Flowers have an attractive pinkish flush at the base. Suits north facing and exposed sites.

'Elsa Späth'. Height 2-3m/6-10ft. Has masses of deep mauve-blue, single flowers throughout summer.

C. montana 'Elizabeth' reaches a height of 10-12m/30-40ft and bears soft pink, scented flowers.

C. macropetala 'Markham's Pink' has delicate, bell-shaped dusky pink flowers and grows to a height of 3m/10ft.

'Nelly Moser' has large, single, flat, rose coloured flowers with a carmine stripe on each petal. It reaches a height of 3.5m/11ft.

C. orientalis has deep yellow, bell-shaped flowers between late summer and autumn. Grows to 3-6m/10-20ft and requires hard pruning early in the year.

'Vyvyan Pennell' is one of the best doubles. Has lavender or violet flowers with magnificent, golden yellow anthers. Height 2.4-3m/8-10ft.

Harry Smith Collection

Photos Horticultural

The alpine clematis (C. alpina) *is the best choice for very exposed sites. The blooms of 'Frances Rivis' (above left) are enhanced by a cluster of white stamens – looking very much like petals – in the centre.*

'Vyvyan Pennell' produces large, double flowers (above) in early summer, followed by a later flush of single, slightly darker blooms.

The semi-double blooms of C. macropetala *are small, just 5cm/2in across, but make up in numbers what they lack in size (above right).*

The yellow flowers of C. orientalis *(right) appear in late summer.*

a height of 2.4-3m/8-10ft.

'Rouge Cardinale' flowers on new wood only, so it needs hard pruning every year. This lovely variety produces masses of velvety, crimson, single flowers in summer and makes an excellent subject for small gardens, growing to a height of 2.4-3m/8-10ft.

'Henryi' is a vigorous plant that boasts lovely, white, single flowers with handsome, chocolate coloured anthers that contrast well with the petals. Flowers appear in summer on a plant that reaches a height of 3m/10ft.

Spring pruning

The third group produces large, flattish flowers in late summer and early autumn. All

'Proteus' is another variety which has a first flush of double flowers with a greenish tint to the outer petals (left), followed by a second of single blooms.

One of the more unusual forms of clematis is C. florida 'Sieboldii' (right), whose flat, star-shaped blooms resemble those of the passion flower. The petals, usually described as creamy-white, can have a green flush, as here, and the central mound is made up of stamens which mature from green to purple.

The crimson petals of 'Rouge Cardinal' (below) have a lovely, soft, velvety texture.

are frost hardy. This group is dominated by 'Jackmanii' varieties. It is very important to prune these annually because the flowers are borne on new growth. For best results, cut them back to the lowest two or three strong buds on each stem in early spring.

C. viticella 'Purpurea Plena Elegans' is a gorgeous variety with double, rose-purple flowers that form tight rosettes. Sometimes the outer petals are green. It reaches a height of 3-4m/10-12ft.

'Jackmanii Superba' grows to about the same height. A vigorous plant, it has large, single, deep purple blooms.

C. florida 'Sieboldii' is really only suitable for a very shel-tered site as it is a bit weak and tender. What it lacks in vigour it makes up for in beauty, however. The flowers are creamy white, with rich, purple stamens. It reaches a height of 2-3m/6-10ft.

Caring for clematis

Clematis like a deep, rich, moist and cool root run. Although they will thrive in almost any good quality, well-cultivated garden soil, good preparation is essential if you want your plant to flower profusely and live long.

Dig a hole 45cm/18in square and deep. Fork over the subsoil at the base and add two or three handfuls of bone meal. Next, add a fairly generous layer of well-rooted manure. Then fill the hole with a mixture of rich garden compost or John Innes No 3, some peat or peat substitute and sand.

Place the crown 5-8cm/2-3in below soil level, burying the first pair of leaves or nodes. Top off with tiles, stones or a thick mulch to keep roots cool and to retain moisture.

Feeding time

Clematis are hungry plants and it pays to feed them regularly as they will soon exhaust the nutrients provided at

GROWING TIPS

HOT HEADS

Many clematis like their feet in the shade and their heads in the sun. All of them like cool roots; place tiles, stones or slates around the stems to keep the ground cool.

Although it is not essential for their well-being, clematis like lime. Covering the roots with a piece of limestone allows some of the mineral to leech into the ground.

planting. Mulch with farmyard manure in autumn or work in some bone meal around the stem. Provide sulphate of potash in spring and feed with a liquid fertilizer every two weeks during the growing season.

Make sure that your plant never goes thirsty by watering during dry spells and by providing a good, thick layer of mulch to prevent the evaporation of precious water from the soil when the sun shines.

Support your clematis

Clematis require support. They do not attach themselves to walls the way ivy does, but twine, so they need something to twine around, either another, preferably woody, plant or an artificial support.

When you wish to clothe a wall or fence, use a trellis or a framework of 23cm/9in squares made with plastic covered wire. Make sure that there is a gap of 1cm/½in between the support and the wall. When planting, allow a gap of at least 30cm/1ft between the clematis and the wall.

If you want a clematis to scramble through a tree, plant it outside the overhang of the branches on the north side.

Bridge the gap between your clematis and the wall or tree with a cane, placed at an angle, so that the plant may twine its way along it to its permanent support.

PERFECT PARTNERS

Photos Horticultural

The twining habit of clematis makes them adept at climbing through other plants.

Here, C. × jackmanii 'Superba' is supported by a double shrub rose.

Luscious Honeysuckles

Sweet honeysuckle instantly evokes images of a country hedgerow. So easy to grow, this delightful shrub will fill your garden with its heady scent all summer.

Harry Smith

Surely every cottage garden has a honeysuckle (lonicera), spreading a fragrant scent and attracting bees? If you want to bring a breath of country air into your garden, there couldn't be a simpler way than to plant a shrub or climbing honeysuckle. This beautiful plant is easy to grow and the vigorous forms will give an attractive show even in their first year.

Most varieties are hardy, and happy in any well-drained soil. All honeysuckles are perennial, so they will give you pleasure year after year. There are many varieties of honeysuckle from which to choose and a whole host of exciting things that can be done with them.

Shrubs and climbers

Some varieties are energetic climbers and may be used to camouflage or soften the lines of sheds, garages and fences. They can be trained to frame

This hybrid honeysuckle, L. × americana (above) will grow vigorously to cloak a wall or fence with its fragrant flowers and glossy foliage. To control it, either prune after flowering or cut off the old stems in winter.

The flowers of L × americana (left), a pretty combination of pink and yellow, stand out well against their background of dark green leaves and their heady fragrance will fill the garden all summer long.

Andrew Lawson

Peter McHoy

PLANT PROFILE

Deciduous, semi-evergreen or evergreen shrubs and climbers with pretty, often very fragrant flowers. The perfect choice for clothing ugly walls, they will grow energetically providing camouflage in a year or two.

Suitable site and soil: sun or light shade in any well-drained, fertile soil, Add well-rotted manure, compost or bone meal at planting time and water in well. Add some sand if your soil tends to retain water.

Cultivation and care: prune climbers after flowering with shears, taking out any rampant, unruly trailers. Prune shrub varieties only to remove dead wood or hold back growth. Feed annually in winter or early spring.

Propagation: root semi-ripe cuttings (when the tip of the stem is still soft and green) towards the end of summer when growth is still strong. Alternatively, take hardwood cuttings (when the stem is hard and woody) in autumn. Stems that run along the ground will multiply naturally by 'layering'.

Pests and diseases: can be prone to aphids.

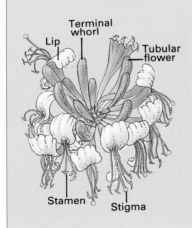

Terminal whorl
Lip
Tubular flower
Stamen
Stigma

This Japanese honeysuckle, L. japonica 'Halliana' (above) is a very vigorous climber, while L. periclymenum 'Belgica' (right), a variety of the common European honeysuckle or woodbine, can actually be quite invasive. Choose L. × brownii (below) with its brilliant red trumpets if you want a really bright splash of colour.

Photos Horticultural

Eric Crichton

your front door or to cover an arch or pergola and will happily grow up walls as long as they are given some support.

Other varieties come in shrub form and can be used to brighten dull spots in your garden. One variety, *Lonicera nitida* can be trained to make a hedge that is an attactive change from privet.

Some shrubs and climbing varieties are evergreen, giving you foliage in the winter months. Others are deciduous.

The best place to grow

Your first tasks are to decide whether you want a climber or a shrub and to choose where

Box honeysuckle, L. nitida, grows vigorously to form a dense evergreen bush that will tolerate wind and salt spray. The variety 'Baggesen's Gold' has yellowy-green foliage. Left to form a natural shaped bush (above), it will brighten up even a shady corner of your garden. Grown as a hedge, it can be clipped to form a neat border on either side of a path or steps.

soil retains water, dig some sand into your site before planting. This will help moisture to drain through and prevent waterlogging.

Some popular climbers

L. americana is a good buy. The flowers are rose-purple in bud, turning creamy white as they open. It grows extremely rapidly, and can reach 9m/30ft if allowed to grow up and over a trellis. It is happiest adorning a west or east-facing wall.

L. periclymenum is also known as the woodbine or Dutch honeysuckle. There are two types from which to choose: early and late. The early variety, 'Belgica', blooms in early summer and then again at summer's end, while 'Serotina' flowers for just one period in early autumn.

These two varieties are such fast growers and are so hardy that many experts think they are the best of the climbers to buy. The woodbine can often be seen growing wild, and it is more resistant to pests and diseases than the more highly bred forms.

Both the early and the late flowering woodbine grow to

you want to put it. It is important to choose the variety which best fulfils your requirements, and suits the situation you have chosen.

The site will need very little preparation and the planning procedure is the same as for many shrubs and climbers. Add well-rotted manure or compost and some bone meal to the bottom of the hole and place your honeysuckle in position, gently teasing out its roots. Replace the soil and firm it down around your plant, then water well.

Although honeysuckles are not too fussy, they do appreciate good drainage. If your

HEALTHY AND HAPPY

To keep your plant healthy, there is no need to use pesticides and other chemicals, providing you follow certain golden rules.

● Buy the healthiest looking specimen you can find, checking the leaves and roots carefully.

● Cut down possible slug and snail damage by making sure you get rid of garden debris – pests quickly set up home in discarded plant pots.

● Be vigilant: at the first sign of aphids, spray with soapy water.

● Keep checking your plant: at the first sign of disease, prune out diseased parts and burn them.

GO ORGANIC!

Andrew Lawson

away from full sun.

L. japonica 'Aureo-reticulata' is a variegated, evergreen climber whose leaves are mottled with gold. The flowers are scented and appear in summer months. It is hardy and will enjoy a sunny or semi-sunny aspect.

Other climbers have distinctive features. *L. henryi* is an evergreen that grows to about 4.5m/15ft and has small flowers followed by glossy

about 4.5m/15ft and this makes them ideal for growing over arches and pergolas as well as up walls and fences. The flowers appear in large clusters and are beautifully scented. They range from creamy white to vibrant yellow with pink or crimson buds and tubes.

It is a good idea to plant both varieties together in order to extend the flowering time. Both enjoy partial shade and are ideally placed facing

Chinese woodbine, L. tragophylla (above), has very large, showy flowers. All climbing honeysuckles have pretty, fragrant flowers such as these creamy 'Early Dutch' blossoms (right), while some varieties also have particularly attractive foliage, especially the yellow-veined leaves of L. japonica 'Aureo-reticulata' (below).

Eric Crichton

Harry Smith

black berries *L. × brownii* is a semi-evergreen which is less vigorous than *L. × americana* and rather delicate. Its blooms are beautiful orange-scarlet.

Some popular shrubs

L. nitida is the type to use for hedging. It is evergreen, with small, neat leaves and creamy-white flowers. During the first two years of growth you will need to clip the hedge often to ensure that it forms a good bushy shape. After that, routine clipping as necessary is all that is required.

'Baggesen's Gold', a variety of *L. nitida*, is a slow growing shrub with decorative, golden leaves. The flowers are yellowish-green and are insignificant next to the foliage. It is just the plant to put in a corner that needs something striking to brighten it up. *L. syringantha* is a deciduous shrub with pale lilac flowers and a very strong scent.

Pruning and feeding

Prune honeysuckle by cutting away flowering shoots after flowering has finished.

A FRIENDLY ENVIRONMENT

Honeysuckle is a must for any 'green' garden. Its heady perfume attracts the insects that a well-balanced garden needs. Some of these friendly visitors help with pollination because they carry pollen on their back legs. Others feed on pests such as aphids.

GO ORGANIC!

PERFECT PARTNERS

Remove dead shoots if and when they appear. If the plant shows signs of getting unruly, cut away any shoots or tendrils that are making a nuisance of themselves. This may be done at any time, though after flowering is generally best. There are no special skills needed for pruning honeysuckle, so just snip away!

Feeding it up

Feed your honeysuckle every year by giving it a top dressing of well-rotted manure, or garden compost and a handful of bone meal. Add water at this stage so that the food finds its way through the soil to the roots more quickly.

This may be done at the beginning of winter or in very early spring. (Follow the maker's instructions when using any fertilizer, organic or chemical.)

For a stunning floral display combine complimentary climbers and grow clematis and honeysuckle together. Both are vigorous climbers and are very easy to grow. Pretty pink C. 'Ville de Lyon' (above) has flower centres that echo the colour and texture of the honeysuckle blossoms, while C. 'Lasurstern' (below) provides a brilliant colour contrast to honeysuckle, *L.x tellmanniana.*

PLANTING POINTS

● Plant deciduous honeysuckle in the autumn and evergreen varieties in spring or autumn.
● Container-grown honeysuckles are best because the roots are not damaged by being dug up and they can be planted at any time.
● As a general rule, honeysuckles like their heads in sun and their roots in shade, but check when buying as some varieties are happy in semi-shade.

GROWING TIPS

Andrew Lawson

Wall-trained Fruit Trees

Turn your fences and walls into a mini-orchard. Planted with fan, cordon or espalier-trained fruit trees, they make attractive – and productive – garden features.

Conventional fruit trees, even those on modern dwarfing rootstocks, take up too much space for most small gardens. Think how much better a flat tree would fit in.

Wall-trained trees are just that. They are trained flush to the wall, with no branches sticking out to obstruct a path, or get in the way in the middle of a lawn or flower bed.

If you do not have a spare wall, then a fence – or even a row of 2m/6ft posts with four horizontal wires stretched between them – will provide a good, sturdy support.

Cordon and espalier trees, trained on posts and wires, can be used to create 'fruiting hedges'. These are a handy way to divide a vegetable garden from the main ornamental garden, or to give height to the back of a border. But remember to leave a path for ease of pruning and picking.

The benefits

Wall-trained fruit trees may not give as much fruit as a full-sized conventional tree, but

A mature fan-trained apple tree graces an old stone garden wall. New shoots have been tied to inconspicuous wires running the length of the wall. The tree is fruiting heavily and the bulk of the apples can be picked from the ground.

TREE SHAPES

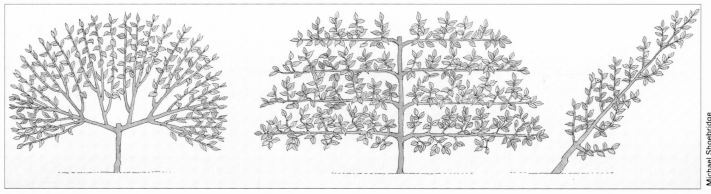

Fan trees are grown on vigorous rootstocks. The branches radiate out.

Espalier trees have a central stem and symmetrical, parallel branches.

Cordon trees take the least space with their short fruit spurs.

the trained tree is more compact. You actually get more fruit per square metre/yard from trained trees, because the method of pruning encourages the production of fruit buds on clusters of twigs.

The other bonus with trained fruit is that, since it takes up less space, you have room to grow a bigger range of varieties. So, in place of a single apple tree, you could grow a fan-trained peach, half a dozen different cordon-trained apples, with fruit ripening from late summer onwards, and a couple of cordon pears.

Apart from the obvious benefit, this also improves pollination. A single tree in a small garden may not have a suitable pollinator tree growing nearby, and will only give a poor crop – or none at all – despite flowering well. By growing several varieties, the chances of good pollination, and therefore good crops, are obviously far better.

Choosing tree shapes

The three basic shapes for wall-trained fruit trees are fans, cordons or espaliers.

Cordons are the most compact if space is really limited. They are also the fastest to start cropping since it does not take long to form their shape.

Fans and espaliers are more decorative, but take longer to train into shape initially. For this reason, it is a good idea to

Neil Holmes

SUITABLE ROOTSTOCKS

M9 – apple. Very dwarfing; makes a weak root system. Trees on M9 need firm supports, regular feeding and watering, and bare soil round them.
M26 – apple. Moderately dwarfing; probably the best rootstock for most trained apples in small gardens.
Quince C – pear. Slightly dwarfing; for cordon and espalier-trained trees.
St Julien A – peaches, nectarines. Slightly dwarfing; for fan-trained trees.
Colt – cherries. Semi-dwarfing rootstock, for fan-trained trees.
Pixy – plums. Semi-dwarfing rootstock, for fan-trained trees.

Eric Crichon

A 'Conference' pear tree trained as an espalier along a wooden fence (above).

Young apple trees in blossom (left). They are cordon-trained.

Fine 'James Grieve' apples on a cordon (right). This is a good eating apple.

A 'Stella' cherry (below), fan-trained on a wattle fence. The branches are being trained along bamboo canes.

buy them already trained (when they start cropping within a year or two), but plants will be more expensive.

Cordons

Cordons have a single stem, usually growing on the slant, from which fruit spurs (short branching clusters of twigs) grow, and carry the crop.

Cordon training is mostly used for apples and pears growing on moderately dwarfing rootstocks.

Cordon trees can be bought already trained, and should start cropping lightly the year after planting. Pruning is done in midsummer.

The idea is to trim the new shoots growing from the fruiting spurs back to 2.5-5cm/1-2in of their base. This is just above the point where the clusters of fruit are developing. (See project box).

You can save a few pounds by training your own cordons. It is quite easy, and they take two years to start cropping. (See project box).

Espaliers

Espalier training is generally used for apples and pears. Espaliers have a single upright trunk from which two or maybe three pairs of branches grow opposite each other, spaced 60cm/2ft or so apart, at right angles to the trunk.

Each branch is rather like a cordon tree, but it grows horizontally. It has fruiting spurs along its length like a cordon, and each branch is pruned in exactly the same way as a complete cordon tree.

Forming the shape of an espalier takes several years and requires regular attention. It is best to buy young

Photos Horticultural

PROJECT

TRAINING CORDON TREES

1 Fix four horizontal wires spaced 45cm/18in apart to a wall, fence or row of posts.
2 Buy 1-2 year old maiden trees in winter. Plant them 75cm/30in apart, at an angle of 45 degrees to the ground.
3 Support each trunk with a 2.4m/8ft cane pushed into the ground for 30cm/1ft. Tie the trunk at intervals of 30-45cm/12-18in.
4 Cut back any laterals (sideshoots) to 10cm/4in from the trunk when you plant the tree.

THE FIRST YEAR

5 In spring, remove any flowers that appear, to allow the tree to establish and develop its shape.
6 'Summer prune' in midsummer. Cut back any new laterals to 10cm/4in as before, and shorten sublaterals (sideshoots arising from existing sideshoots) to 2.5-5cm/1-2in from their base, just above the clusters of young, developing fruit.
7 When the leaves fall, cut back all the new growth that has appeared since summer pruning to 2.5cm/1in from its base, again cutting just above a bud. This will build up lots of fruiting spurs which will carry the crop.

FOLLOWING YEARS

8 In second spring, remove premature flowers, leaving basal rosettes, to discourage early fruiting. Summer prune each year. When the fruiting spurs become densely branched, thin them out in winter by removing weak growths, leaving strong, well-spaced shoots.

Michael Shoebridge

Photos Horticultural

ready-trained trees from a nursery. These should start fruiting the second summer after planting.

If space is short, you can buy espalier trees in which each branch is a separate variety; a 'family' tree. You can get family apple trees and family pears – but not on the same tree.

A family tree can be very useful if you only have room for one wall-tree, as the varieties used are carefully chosen to cross-pollinate each other. Between them they will produce a succession of fruit, ripening over a long period.

Fans

Fan-trained trees have their branches radiating out in a traditional fan shape from the base of the plant.

This form of training needs a fairly vigorous plant. It is commonly used for fruit for which no really dwarfing rootstocks are as yet available. These include plums, peaches, nectarines, apricots, almonds and cherries.

Since these fruits need warmth to ripen properly, they do best grown against a south-facing wall or fence. Except in very mild, sheltered areas, they do not do well grown on posts and wires situated out in the open.

Growing the trees against a wall or fence also makes it much easier to protect them from birds. Just nail a batten along the top of the wall, tack bird netting to it and drape it down over the trees as the fruit starts to ripen.

Fan-trained 'Rochester' peaches protected by netting from the birds (above). The netting has been fixed to the top of the fence and draped down.

Tree nurseries train fruit trees so that gardeners can buy them ready-trained. These pear trees (left) are being trained as cordons.

The 'Morello' cherry (below) flowers late and is suitable for a north wall. This variety is self-fertile.

Some people even build a permanent wooden framework over which nets can be draped for the fruiting season.

Like espaliers, training a fan from scratch takes several years and is quite complicated. It is far better to buy a young tree whose basic shape has already been formed.

Routine pruning is then keeping it in shape, and periodically renewing old fruiting branches with young vigorous shoots. (See box).

Any fairly sheltered site can be used for trained fruit, provided the soil is fertile and not waterlogged in winter or strongly acid or alkaline.

Orientation

A south- or west-facing wall is really best for most fruit. East-facing walls should be avoided since fruit flowers early in the season when there is a risk of late frosts. If the early morning sun shines directly onto frozen flowers they are killed and the crop is lost for that year. North-facing walls can however be used to grow 'Morello' (cooking) cherries.

GROWING TIPS

ROUTINE PRUNING OF FAN TREES

Late winter – cut back the main shoots that make up the 'ribs' of the fan by one third. Prune to just above a bud.

Bud-burst – in spring, when growth buds start to develop, prune back to the base any sideshoots that are growing in towards the wall or outwards over the path.

Summer – tie new shoots in to the wall (using wall nails, or use string to tie them to trellis). The idea is to fill in any gaps that may have developed in the fan pattern.

Replacing old branches – after several years, when the wall is completely covered with branches, start replacing a few of the oldest branches with vigorous young shoots.

Choose one strong shoot growing from the base of each of the branches to be replaced and mark it with a piece of coloured ribbon.

After the fruit have been picked (in the case of peaches, apricots and nectarines), or in winter (plums) or when the buds start to burst in spring (cherries), prune the old fruited shoot back to just above the shoot you have left. Then tie the new shoot into place.

Versatile Ivies

Ivy is one of the most versatile evergreen garden plants, providing a range of foliage shapes, colours and textures to set off its autumn flowers and fruits.

Eric Crichton

Ivy's natural tendency to creep and climb make it a perfect choice for ground cover or to clothe a wall or shed. Its long trailing shoots are particularly pleasing tumbling from window boxes or hanging baskets. It is also much enjoyed as an indoor plant.

Ivy is a woody perennial plant that can live for many hundreds of years. It has two distinct phases of growth. Young or juvenile ivy, with deeply indented or lobed leaves, is most commonly found in gardens. It scrambles along the ground or climbs, using small aerial roots that grow from its stems to anchor it to supports.

The next phase in its growth, when it has reached sufficient height and light, is to develop slightly oval, entire leaves. The stems become thicker and no aerial roots are present. In autumn, the plant produces umbels of tiny, greeny-white flowers, followed by black berries.

This mature form, known as tree or arborescent ivy, can be grown as an independent shrub or allowed to continue growing as a scrambling plant, making dense cover on trees and walls.

There are seven species of

GROWING TIPS

SLOW STARTERS

Young ivy plants are usually slow growing in their first year in the ground. Do not over-fertilize them at this stage. Keep them well-watered and in their second year top dress with granular fertilizer.

Hedera helix 'Buttercup', H. colchica and H. canariensis 'Variegata' (above) combine to make an attractive, dense wall cover.

All ivies produce small black fruits in autumn (above right) with the exception of H. helix 'Poetica' which bears glorious yellow berries.

One of the most popular climbers is the delightful H. helix 'Goldheart' (right), with its splashy yellow centres.

Gillian Beckett

ivy, including common ivy (*Hedera helix*), which has over 300 varieties. Varieties of common ivy can themselves be divided into groups. Ivies that produce long, unbranched trails are described as vining, and are best used as climbers. The second group, self-branching ivies, produce branching shoots along the main stems, and are suitable for ground cover and for growing in containers both indoors and outside.

Uncommonly versatile

Common ivy, a favourite for use in seasonal festive door wreaths, is one of the best choices for glossy, evergreen ground and wall cover. It quickly covers unsightly tree stumps and lends an air of romantic antiquity to corners

Brian Carter/Garden Picture Library

PLANT PROFILE

Suitable site and soil Ivy's woodland origin is a guide to the site and soil in which it thrives; partial shade, with a cool root run under a mulch of leaves or compost. Ivies with variegated leaves need more light and may be less hardy in severe conditions. All ivies grow best in well-drained fertile soils.

Planting Plant container-grown ivies at any time, although spring and autumn are generally best. Dig a hole larger than the root-ball, water well and add well-rotted organic matter or a handful of bone meal. Spread roots out into the hole, and firm the plant in.

Cultivation and care Water thoroughly in dry conditions. If growing ivy against a wall or other support, tie in the longest shoots to encourage climbing. Apply liquid fertilizer in the growing period. Trim from time to time to encourage new growth. Variegated and coloured leaf ivies do not respond well to regular trimming.

All ivies can be cut back once they have reached the desired height and spread. Cut out any shoots that revert to green on variegated plants and, if you do not want the mature tree ivy form to develop, cut this out, too, as it appears.

Propagation Take cuttings from new growth from early summer through to autumn. Each cutting should have at least three leaves. Remove the lower leaf and pot up to just below the leaf node. Use a well-draining mixture of sand and two parts peat for cuttings.

Insert the cuttings around the edge of a 9cm/ 3½in pot and cover with a plastic bag. Keep in a humid place out of direct sun for three weeks.

Alternatively, layer ivy stems on the ground or into pots. It will be at least four weeks before you can cut new ivy from the parent plant.

Pests and diseases Mainly trouble free, but in hot, dry conditions red spider mite is likely. Scale insects and aphids are found on indoor and wall-grown ivies. Leaf spot and powdery mildew may occur in damp conditions.

WILDLIFE HAVEN

Ivy on trees and walls provides a shelter and a larder for birds and insects. It is not a parasite so will not harm its tree support.

On old and leafless trees, ivy provides birds with good nesting cover in spring and berries for food in winter. In autumn its flowers provide nectar for butterflies, wasps and drowsy bees, while its flowers and berries provide food for the caterpillars of the holly blue butterfly.

where it is allowed to scramble and climb freely.

In dense shade, under trees, where little else would grow satisfactorily, common ivy will provide a glimmering green cover to suppress most tough annual weeds.

Ivy is also one of the most popular indoor plants, known for its ability to tolerate low light levels and any amount of neglect. Recently it has acquired a reputation as a purifer of polluted office air. Its attractive foliage has long been popular for the way it softens and warms interiors.

As a wall plant, ivy is very accommodating, as it does best on difficult north, east or west

Hedera helix 'Glacier' (right) is a favourite ground-cover ivy. It is notably hardy and its variegated silver-grey leaves are particularly attractive.

The romantic associations of the heart-shaped leaves of H. helix 'Deltoidea' (far right), combined with its stiff stems, make it a popular choice for flower arrangers.

H. colchica 'Sulphur Heart' (below right) is equally at home as a climber or as ground cover. Its large variegated leaves have a central splash of colour.

RECOMMENDED VARIETIES

Climbers
Hedera azorica 'Typica' is very hardy, fast-growing with large matt green leaves.

H. canariensis 'Gloire de Marengo' (also sold as 'Variegata') is fast-growing. Has creamy-white edges to its elegant leaves.

H. colchica 'Dentata' has large, unlobed leaves. Its variegated forms, 'Dentata Variegata' and 'Sulphur Heart', have attractive colouring and are good climbers, but need supporting.

Hedera helix 'Buttercup' needs a sunny position. 'Glymii' is dark purple in winter and a good climber. 'Goldheart', with green edges to its golden-centred leaves, is a hardy climber that needs no support.

Ground cover
'Glacier' has silver-grey foliage. Hardy and good indoors as well. 'Brokamp' has willow-like, medium-sized leaves. One of the few ivies to remain bright green in winter. 'Deltoidea' has heart-shaped leaves that turn to bronze in winter.

Containers
'Kolibri' has white speckled leaves and trails prettily. 'Adam' has creamy-white leaf edges that turn to pink in winter. 'Midas Touch' has wavy golden variegation and needs a sheltered position. 'Poetica' is a very old ivy, grown mostly as a mature tree ivy for its yellow berries. Grow it in a container for a few years then plant it out as a specimen shrub.

walls, leaving precious south-facing walls free for more sun-loving climbers.

It is usually quite slow growing in its first year, but once settled it will race ahead. It may need tying in or staking to encourage it in the direction you wish it to climb. Some of the larger-leaved ivies are too heavy to support themselves, and will need a permanent support system.

A large canvas

This may be a practical disadvantage, but in decorative terms means you can provide colour and cover on the same scale as a big wall surface. Persian ivy (*Hedera colchica*), with its wide, almost handkerchief-shaped leaves, suits such a large canvas. The variety 'Dentata' (elephant's ears), and its variegated forms 'Dentata Variegata' and 'Sulphur Heart', need support to

Gillian Beckett

Photos Horticultural

BRIGHT IDEAS

GET INTO SHAPE

Ivy is great fun to use as an inexpensive topiary plant. It can quickly be trained into hoops, cones and whimsical animal shapes. Use coat hangers and chicken wire to make the supporting frames. On a patio make an ivy-encrusted basket frame to hold bright summer bedding plants.

low leaves, are less hardy. In severe winters they will be damaged by wind and frost, though the plants will survive.

For best colouring, plant variegated ivy such as 'Glacier', 'Anne Marie' or 'Chester' where it gets good dappled sunlight. For green ground cover, choose 'Dragon Claw', with its deeply waved leaves, or 'Brokamp', which has light green angular foliage.

Useful as a climber or trail-

ing from a container, sweetheart ivy (*H. helix* 'Deltoidea') is undoubtedly best as a ground cover plant. Its dark green, almost heart-shaped leaves deepen to a purplish hue in winter. Its rather stiff stems make it a popular choice for flower arrangers.

Ivy contained

Cascades of delicate, smaller-leaved green and variegated ivy trailing from hanging bas-

start but once growing well will provide a generous splash of colour and shine to lighten a bare wall.

For well-defined, bright pools of sunlight yellow on a north facing wall, use *H. helix* 'Goldheart', whose green-edged leaves have a strong yellow centre. The sunniest of all ivies, the beautiful 'Buttercup', needs full sun to perform at its best, producing marble-textured, entirely yellow leaves, although young plants are likely to be green.

On the level

There are both green and variegated ivies suitable for ground cover, but variegated ivies, especially those with yel-

Harry Smith Collection

PERFECT PARTNERS

Eric Crichton

Hedera helix 'Buttercup' can make a wonderful backdrop for climbing flowers but few combinations are as happy as this one, interwoven with the pretty *Rosa* 'Bantry Bay'.

UPRIGHT IVY

H. helix 'Erecta', known as candelabra ivy, is self-supporting and upright in its growth habit. It has rather cupped leaves and will grow to 1.2m/4ft high, making a useful garden feature at the foot of a low wall.

kets and window boxes can provide year-round pleasure. Whether they are used with annual summer plants or with spring bulbs, ivies offer an exuberant show, softening and adding line and texture to container displays.

There are many varieties to choose from, including 'Kolibri' with its white speckled leaves. It is equally at home grown in containers in or outside. 'Adam' with creamy-white leaf edges that turn pinkish in winter, looks attractive trailing from terracotta urns or window boxes. 'Midas Touch' with its golden variegation can make a very rich splash of colour, given a sheltered position. For unusually shaped green leaves, use 'Fluffy Ruffles' or 'Manda's Crested'.

In winter the leaves of some ivies deepen from green to bronze, while others turn a rich purple. 'Atropurpurea' (also known as 'Purpurea') and 'Glymii', both good climbing plants, turn a deep purple, while 'Succinata', which has been grown since the 1800s, has bronzed leaves in winter and amber spring growth.

Buy small plants rather

OLD FAITHFUL

Poets' ivy (*Hedera helix* 'Poetica') was known of in Roman times and was then used to make garlands for poets and heroes. It is sought after because of the yellowy-orange berries produced on mature plants. You can buy it as a small tree ivy specimen plant from specialist nurseries.

than large, well-established plants for climbing. Only new growth will cling to supports and wall surfaces and young plants will establish quicker.

To cover a large wall you will need to put your plants about 90cm/3ft apart. For good ground cover you will need one plant for every square metre or square yard.

Looking after ivy

Ivies grow in most soil conditions, but do best if the ground is not heavy. Prepare it by forking it over well and adding well-rotted organic matter. A well-drained soil makes it easier for ivy's deep soil roots to find the necessary nutrients for growth.

As an alternative to adding bulky organic matter, when planting put a slow-release fertilizer on the base of the planting hole.

Although ivy will compete successfully with most annual weeds, give it a good start and remove them from the planting area. Remove perennial weeds too, as ivy will not be able to suppress them.

Water the new plants in and in dry conditions ensure they are well watered until they

settle down. Cover the soil around the plants with a leaf-mould or bark mulch. Ivy in containers must be kept well watered, but, once established, ivy in the ground will be fairly drought resistant.

In spring, scatter granular fertilizer around established plants. Cut out any green shoots on variegated ivies and trim back green ivies when they need controlling.

H. helix 'Manda's Crested' (below) used to be called 'Curly Locks' which describes it well. It can make an attractive container plant or be used as ground cover.

The trailing habit of the speckled, white, variegated ivy, H. helix 'Kolibri' (bottom), makes it a charming plant for hanging baskets or pots.

Though less hardy than non-variegated varieties, variegated ivies, like Hedera colchica 'Dentata Variegata' (facing page), are popular with many gardeners, and are used to brighten gardens.

Colourful Wigwams

For a crop of tasty runner beans or a swathe of colourful sweet peas, try this original and space-saving idea.

To get the most from a small garden you need to use space to maximum advantage. Think of limited space not as a barrier to creative gardening, but as a challenge.

You may not have room for a vegetable garden, but that need not deter you from growing a healthy crop of runner beans or tall-growing peas. A wigwam-shaped structure can be fitted into any small space – the corner of a flower bed, a balcony, patio or even a flat roof garden – and will enable you to grow a number of vegetables or flowering plants.

Getting started

A wigwam is cheap and easy to construct to almost any size. You can use a variety of materials, depending on the size and weight of the plants you want to grow. Bamboo poles, pea sticks and even strong twigs are all suitable.

Wigwams in containers are a good way to expand your garden onto the patio or balcony, creating an unusual feature and adding a touch of colour. Take care in choosing a container that is large enough to support the fully grown plants without toppling over.

Perfect proportions

Your wigwam must be strong enough to support the plants. Make sure it is not so large, though, that the contents will look out of proportion with the container in which it stands.

Very vigorous perennials, like some forms of clematis and rambling roses, make striking features but need strong supports. They are

unsuitable for all but the largest of containers.

Good containers for tall plants include half barrels, deep sinks and troughs. You can also use large plastic pots weighted at the bottom with heavy rocks or broken bricks. Mini-wigwams, which support smaller annual flowers, are ideal for less bulky containers.

In the garden

You can put your wigwam in any area of the garden large enough to house a circle of a minimum of 75cm/2ft 6in in diameter. Use your wigwam constructively and situate it where it will hide an eyesore like a garden shed or compost bin. Bear in mind that once the plants are growing strongly your wigwam will take on a

GROWING TIPS

BE CREATIVE

● Mix and match – runner beans and sweet peas can look good together or try different annuals on the same wigwam.
● Runner beans don't always have red flowers. Look out for pink 'Sunset', white 'Desiree' or even red and white 'Painted Lady'. Grow them separately or together.
● The runner bean 'Purple Podded' is pretty and delicious.
● Experiment with different shaped wigwams — ovals, triangles or rectangles. Don't bend each cane too much however as it may snap. If you can't gather the canes at the top try tying them to a short horizontal cane.

Andrew Lawson

Wigwams are a great space saver in the vegetable garden. These tall bamboo structures (above) are not only bound at the top, they also have strings wound round them in a spiral from top to bottom, to provide added support for peas and beans.

solid appearance. So when you select the position try to place it behind smaller plants.

When your wigwam is thickly covered in foliage, rain will have difficulty getting to the centre so give the plants regular long drinks.

First decide what you want to grow up your wigwam. For

and help to prevent your beans drying out in hot weather. Then dig in some well-rotted manure or garden compost to enrich the ground.

Water your bean plants twice a week throughout the flowering and pod-growing season, directing the water at the base of the plants and not at the flowers and foliage. Adequate watering is essential to produce a good crop, but do not keep the soil saturated as it could cause root rot.

Round in circles

The size of your wigwam will depend on what you grow up it. For beans and larger perennials use 2-2.5m/7-8ft heavy grade bamboo canes which will support the weight of these fairly heavy plants. Place one upright in the centre and arrange the others in a circle around it, 15-30cm/6-12in apart. Push the ends firmly into the ground and tie

These sweet peas (above) will grow right to the top of this 1.5m/5ft wigwam, making a pretty and compact display, as well as providing a good stock of flowers for cutting.

annual or perennial flowers simply dig the ground over and add a little general fertilizer. If you choose climbing French or runner beans, prepare the ground by digging it over and placing layers of wet newspapers about 45cm/18in below the surface. These will hold moisture when you water

Here is positive proof that a wigwam can be used for a decorative as well as a practical purpose. A container-grown clematis (left) can be trained into a neat, conical shape with just a bit of prudent pruning.

75

A CLEMATIS COVERED WIGWAM

1 Drill holes, using a large 0.8cm/¹/₂in bit, approximately 15cm/6in apart in the base of a wooden half-barrel.

2 Cover base with a layer of drainage material, such as broken pots, to prevent soil blocking the holes.

3 Fill to within 3cm/1¹/₂ in of the rim with a suitable compost such as John Innes No. 3. Do not use garden soil.

4 Tease out the roots of the clematis and plant it in a hole deep enough to cover the first two buds.

5 Push hazel sticks into the soil. Choose lengths appropriate to the mature height of the plant.

6 Tie in the stems of the clematis to the stakes using garden twine and taking care not to tie too tightly.

7 Tie the sticks together at the top to create the wigwam shape. Use twine or proprietary holders if using bamboo.

8 Give the container a thorough soaking using a fine rose. Water regularly in the first few weeks.

9 A layer of grit will improve the look of the tub, prevent earth splashing up during watering and retain moisture.

Marshall Cavendish

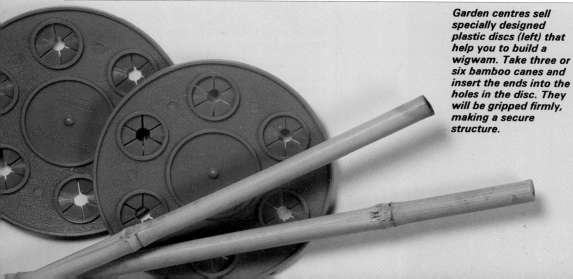

Garden centres sell specially designed plastic discs (left) that help you to build a wigwam. Take three or six bamboo canes and insert the ends into the holes in the disc. They will be gripped firmly, making a secure structure.

will normally be enough.

Plant one bean to each pole. As they grow tie them loosely to the framework of the wigwam and, when they are long enough, twist them anti-clockwise around the pole. Beans prefer a sunny spot and should be harvested regularly to keep them cropping. Snap off pods cleanly so as not to damage the plant.

Hedges to Please Everyone

Hedges can do more than mark the boundaries of a garden. Use them to create patterns and secret spaces, protect plants – even deter burglars!

It may just be a collection of shrubs or trees growing together to make a living screen, but a hedge can provide a range of creative possibilities for your garden.

Hedges are used to form physical boundaries between properties. In a front garden, they often mark the limits between public and private ground. If a hedge is very high it will provide privacy from neighbouring houses or passers-by; it may lower noise levels from a nearby road or school playground and it can even keep stray animals out. It will also provide shelter and protect your garden plants from strong winds.

Part of the design

As well as these practical functions, however, hedges also play a decorative role and can be an essential part of your garden design. To increase your enjoyment of your garden there are many ways you can get both practical value and

Photos Horticultural

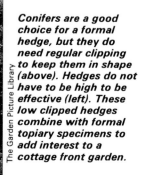

Conifers are a good choice for a formal hedge, but they do need regular clipping to keep them in shape (above). Hedges do not have to be high to be effective (left). These low clipped hedges combine with formal topiary specimens to add interest to a cottage front garden.

The Garden Picture Library

Andrew Lawson

good looks from a hedge.

Hedges can be grown for either a formal or an informal look. Traditionally, formal hedges are made from plantings of evergreen shrubs including yew, box and privet.

These evergreens look the same all year round, which gives them their unchanging, formal character. All three plants respond well to regular clipping into a trim shape. They are all hardy and long-lived and provide a rich foliage backdrop for the other plants in the garden.

The informal look

If you want a hedge that is more relaxed in form then choose plants that suit an informal look. *Skimmia japonica*, an evergreen shrub with gold-spotted leaves and autumn berries, is a good choice. For a flush of spring flowers in your informal hedge choose *Forsythia × intermedia* 'Spectabilis'. For summer flowers choose *Potentilla arbuscula*. All will make loose hedges but will provide a screen, offer privacy or mark a boundary.

If you want to attract birds to the garden, *Cotoneaster* 'Cornubia' and *Pyracantha rogersiana* will provide you with evergreen foliage, summer flowers and autumn berries for the birds to enjoy.

In coastal areas two shrubs are invaluable both as ornamental and practical hedge plants: *Escallonia macrantha* with its red to pink summer flowers, and *Griselinia littoralis,* with its fresh green foliage. Both tolerate salty winds.

Mix and match

Instead of using one type of shrub or tree for the hedge, you can create a very informal effect by planting different species. The overall impression will be of a highly textured surface. Hornbeam, holly, beech and laurel can be mixed together to create this type of look but it will take time as they are long-lived but

slow-growing plants.

If you wish to make a wild-life garden and attract birds and butterflies, plant a native hedgerow of sloe, hawthorn, holly and hazel. Plant native climbers such as honeysuckle, wild clematis and hop at intervals along the hedge.

Ring the colour changes with an informal hedge. The foliage of beech (above right) is a bright green in spring, which matures to a darker green before assuming rich russet tones in the autumn. Beech also holds its leaves through the winter until new growth starts in spring. Some forms of berberis (right) also produce spectacular autumn colours.

Peter McHoy

GOOD HEDGING PLANTS

Plant (suggested hedge height)	Planting distance	Cultivation and care
Barberry (Berberis x stenophylla) 1.3-1.8m/4-6ft	75cm/30in	Use this evergreen to make an informal hedge. It produces yellow flowers in spring and berries in autumn. Trim after flowering or in autumn.
Beech (Fagus sylvatica) 1.3-1.8m/4-6ft hedge	45cm/18in	A deciduous tree for formal hedges, it holds its old leaves through most of the winter, then produces a flush of young leaves in spring. Trim in autumn.
Cotton lavender (Santolina chamaecyparissus) 60cm/2ft	30cm/12in	Use this evergreen plant with its bright yellow flowers in summer for a low formal hedge or edging around a herb garden. Trim lightly in spring or after flowering.
Firethorn (Pyracantha rogersiana) 1.3-1.8m/4-6ft	75cm/30in	An evergreen, it can be used for informal hedging. Spring flowers are later followed by berries. Trim lightly after flowering, if you want to keep the berries.
Holly (Ilex aquifolium) 1.3-2.5m/4-8ft	90cm/36in	An evergreen shrub, it can be trimmed into a formal shape or allowed to create a more informal hedge. Trim in autumn.
Leyland cypress (× Cupressocyparis leylandii) 1.8-2.5m/6-8ft	105cm/42in	This evergreen grows very fast, and can be used to create a neat, formal hedge. Trim in late summer.
Mexican orange blossom (Choisya ternata) 1.3-1.8m/4-6ft	75cm/30in	This evergreen shrub produces sweet-smelling flowers and makes a largely informal hedge. Trim after flowering.
Privet (Ligustrum ovalifolium) 1-1.8m/3-6ft	45cm/18in	A popular and fast-growing evergreen, it can be trimmed into neat, formal shapes. Clip regularly during the growing season.

Pyracantha (above) makes a very attractive hedge, bearing dense clusters of white flowers in early summer followed by orange-yellow or red fruits. Senecio greyi (left) is particularly suited to coastal areas as it tolerates salt breezes. Privet (right) is one of the most popular hedging plants. This variety, Ligustrum ovalifolium 'Aureo Marginatum', often sold as Aureum, has golden leaves and prefers a sunny spot.

For a more whimsical effect, privet, yew and box hedges can be clipped into specific shapes, such as bird or animal forms. This is known as topiary. Remember, though, that these plants are slow-growing, so the topiary shapes will take some time to achieve. In a dense hedge dividing a garden across its width you might wish to cut a circular or other geometrically shaped window, through which you can view the rest of your garden.

Saftey first

If you want to deter burglars and vandals plant a dense and prickly hedge in a front garden or where there is a vulnerable point of entry to your property. Holly, although slow-growing, will eventually make a painfully impenetrable hedge. Particularly prickly is the hedgehog holly, *Ilex aquifolium* 'Ferox Argentea'.

Roses, lovely to smell and delightful to look at, will also offer a spiky obstacle. *Rosa rugosa* 'Frau Dagmar Hastrup' has very thorny stems, lovely flowers and fat rosehips in autumn. Berberis, with spring flowers, and mahonia, with autumn flowers and purplish berries later, have thorns and spiky leaves.

Create an illusion

As well as providing a screen along the edge of your garden, you can use hedges in other ways. You can make a long, narrow garden feel larger by using hedges to divide it across the width. You can even divide your garden into 'rooms' or compartments that offer changes of mood. Create doorways by arching the hedge plants, or set an iron or wooden trellis archway in place for roses to grow over.

You do not have to use high hedges to gain this effect: a hedge of low-growing plants such as lavender or rosemary can also be used to break up a plot and the aromatic leaves are an added bonus.

Ideas from the past

Low hedges have, in fact, been a traditional garden feature in Britain since Elizabethan times. They are still used to make strongly outlined geometric or floral designs, known as 'knot gardens'. The hedges mark the outline of the design

A FAST HEDGE

One of the quickest-growing hedge plants is the Leyland cypress *(Cupressocyparis × leylandii)*. To make a hedge, follow these simple steps:
- First mark out your straight planting line with string.
- Dig holes large enough to receive the roots of plants at 1m/3ft intervals (the plants will eventually grow to fill the space between).
- Scatter compost in the base of each hole and, if the site is exposed, firm in a stake.
- Place each plant in its hole, cover the roots with soil up to the soil level mark on the stem base, and firm in.
- If you have used stakes, fix the plants to them and, if the site is particularly windy, protect the hedging with a netting windbreak.
- Water regularly until the plants are well-established.

which is best viewed from an upstairs window. Inside the hedge framework, low-growing plants such as violets, marigolds and herbs such as thyme, savory and marjoram are grown to form shapes.

Why not create your own knot garden to frame a selection of summer bedding plants, or to mark out a small herb garden. Use traditional knot garden hedging plants: cotton lavender *(Santolina chamaecyparissus)*, box *(Buxus sempervirens)* or small lavender species.

Protect your plants

A low-growing hedge is particularly useful in a garden where children play regularly. Use it to mark the edge of the lawn – the safest play area for children – and it will protect flowerbeds or vegetable patches from the onslaught of exuberant younger members of the family.

In large, old gardens, hedges were often used in a similar way to keep ornamental areas and productive vegetable areas separate. Few gardens have space for such strict segregation, but if you do want to keep them apart why not grow a specially trained step-over

AN EDIBLE MINI-HEDGE

Divide your herb or vegetable garden into a series of decorative sections using short, bushy salad and herb plants grown close together to form bushy edgings. Good plants to try include:
- chives. Plant closely together.
- lettuce. Choose the 'cut and come again' varieties – the hearting types will not grow into each other and picking your dinner would create a hole in your hedge.
- rosemary. Once established, this can be clipped into shape with shears.
- thyme. Choose from among the compact, bushy types rather than the low mat-forming varieties. Plant fairly close together and clip into shape with shears once established.
- pot marigold *(Calendula officinalis)*. Plant close together to add a splash of colour. The bright colour petals are edible and will add decoration to a summer salad.

Eric Crichton

cordon apple or pear hedge.

On a patio a hedge offers privacy as well as good shelter from prevailing winds. Choose plants that are pretty to look at or have scented, aromatic qualities. Low-growing evergreens such as hebes offer a year-round silvery effect. When you are sitting on the patio the plants may be at eye-level, so choose plants that look attractive from all angles. Mexican orange blossom *(Choisya ternata)* has lovely evergreen leaves with citrus-scented white flowers in

Mixing and matching your plants can result in a very attractive hedge (below). Choose plants that have roughly similar habits and need approximately the same amount of clipping to make your life easier.

spring. Train as a low hedge or use pyramid-shaped formal specimens in tubs lined up to create a neat row.

Make a windbreak

A hedge can also provide the ideal windbreak in a garden. For best wind protection, you need a barrier that allows some wind through. A barrier that blocks the wind completely causes turbulence and gusts that can do as much damage as the wind itself.

A permeable barrier made of hedge plants breaks the

Tania Midgley

HEDGING TERMS

- **Knot garden**: an ornamental design of interlocking shapes, outlined in low hedging and filled with flowers or herbs.
- **Parterre**: a geometric design of beds and narrow pathways, edged with hedges, usually larger than a knot garden and sited near the house so it can be viewed from above.
- **Topiary**: hedges, trees or shrubs clipped into ornamental shapes, for example cones or spirals, the shapes of animals or birds or even more whimsical, individual designs.

A row of small trees or bushes like these junipers (left) serve many of the same purposes as a hedge while letting in more light.

A forsythia hedge (below) offers a lovely flush of spring colour. Cut it back hard after flowering and then leave alone as the following year's flowers are borne on the current year's growth.

shape, it will provide your garden with invaluable shelter.

Hedges also provide winter shelter and a safe haven for many nesting garden birds.

Routine maintenance

When it comes to pruning your hedge, what you do will depend on the type of hedge you have. The practical reason for pruning hedges is to keep the plant producing shoots from its base. After planting a new hedge cut the plants back by at least half. Leave them to grow unpruned for their first growing season; then in the second year, between spring and summer, clip them every four to six weeks, especially if they begin to look a little lax in their growth. Keep the upper part of the hedge slightly narrower than the base. This allows plenty of light to get into the growing shoots at the base of the hedge and, if you are in an area with snowy winters, heavy snows will not break the hedge open and damage it.

Informal hedges need very little maintenance. Prune them at least once a year during the growing season. If the hedge bears autumn fruits do not prune it after flowering; wait until the next spring. Trim flowering hedges after their blooming period is over.

strength of the wind, protecting the plants on the other side of it from a battering. The wind will blow through the leaves and branches of your hedge plants, but its effects will not be so damaging by the time it reaches your ornamental garden plants.

Even though they are deciduous, beech hedges provide a successful windbreak all year round. The spring leaves offer a delightful show of foliage and in winter the young plants hold their wispy brown leaves until the new ones show.

For a quick-growing windbreak, Leyland cypress is the best choice. It needs regular clipping or it will grow too fast, but if you manage it well and keep it clipped into a good

Lavender, like this Lavandula spica 'Hidcote' (above right) makes the ideal hedging for a patio or terrace. You can enjoy its fragrance as you sit and relax while it will not grow tall enough to obscure your view.

Rosa rugosa (right) is a vigorous species rose that carries a succession of fragrant single cupped flowers in summer, followed by large tomato-shaped colourful hips to make a very informal hedge.

Flowering Hedges

Flowering hedges offer a colourful backdrop to a garden in all seasons, offering you rich flowers and greenery as well as many practical benefits.

Your garden needs boundaries, both to mark the limits of your land and to divide off different areas within it. There are many ways to mark these boundaries, but one of the most attractive is to plant a hedge.

Many flowering shrubs make excellent hedging plants, and need very little maintenance once established.

Flowering hedges are not the ideal choice for a very formal garden. Because they are grown for their flowers, and sometimes for their berries, they should be pruned only lightly, sometimes only once a year. As a result, while they can form an impenetrable barrier, it is impossible to achieve a smooth top and sides.

For the gardener with little spare time, however, this low maintenance is a positive advantage, leaving more time for other tasks or for you simply to sit back and enjoy it.

Plan first

Before choosing shrubs for your hedge, you must set your goal. If it is a boundary hedge, should it be decorative, or do you want it thick enough to keep animals and children in or out? Do you want to be shielded from the prying eyes of neighbours or to receive as much light as possible?

You may want a high hedge to screen off the compost bin or vegetable patch, or to create a series of small gardens. Alternatively, a low hedge of 30-45cm/12-18in could separate one area from another without blocking your view of the entire garden. All the

The beautiful mature hedges here are of Berberis stenophylla (top), escallonia (left) and Rosa rugosa (right). A hedge is a long-term collection of shrubs grown in a line. Before planting, look carefully at those that would grow well on your soil and bear in mind that it may be many years before they look their best.

SHRUBS FOR LARGE FLOWERING HEDGES

Name	Description	Distance	Planting tips and maintenance
Berberis x stenophylla	Evergreen, yellow flowers in spring, purple berries in autumn if left untrimmed	45-60cm/ 18-24in	Plant 30-38cm/12-15in plants, autumn or spring. Remove top quarter of shoots for bushy growth. Prefers sun or light shade. Prune once a year, after flowering.
Escallonia macrantha	Evergreen, red flowers summer to early autumn	45cm/18in	Plant 30cm/12in plants in autumn or spring. Remove top quarter of shoots for bushy growth. Thrives in coastal areas. Prune once a year after flowering.
Pyracantha rogersiana (firethorn)	Evergreen, white flowers in early summer, orange-red berries autumn to spring	38-60cm/ 15-24in	Plant autumn to spring. Prune back current season's growth by half. Pinch out growing points of young shoots at 15-20cm/6-8in. Prune with shears late spring/ early summer. Prefers sun or light shade.
Spiraea thunbergii	Deciduous, white flowers appear before leaves in spring	38-60cm/ 15-24in	Plant autumn to spring. Cut back previous season's growth to 15cm/6in above ground. Stop later growths at 7.5-10cm/3-4in. Prune with shears after flowering. Prefers open, sunny position.
Rosa rugosa	Deep pink, scented flowers early summer to autumn, followed by orange-red hips	60cm/24in	Plant autumn to spring. Prune lightly in autumn.

Photos Horticultural

FORWARD PLANNING

GROWING TIPS

Flowering hedges, like all plants, grow better in well-prepared soil. Before planting your shrubs, dig a trench 45cm/18in wide and 30cm/12in deep, incorporating generous amounts of well-rotted compost or manure. Water the young plants regularly until they are established. Remember that you will get more and better flowers if the hedge is in sun or light shade, not in heavy shade.

liage during other seasons.

For a touch of winter colour, consider the different dogwoods (*Cornus*), planted about 90cm/3ft apart. Most are deciduous and will not produce a very dense hedge. But this also means that they let in maximum light during the bare winter months.

Their stems are of striking colours, ranging from maroon to bright red and pale yellowish-green. The bare stems are succeeded by small star-shaped flowers, usually white or yellow, in late spring or early summer, and white berries in the autumn.

Apart from cutting the stems hard back to within a few inches of the ground in the spring, your dogwood hedge will need no further maintenance during the year.

Creating a barrier

The evergreen barberry (*Berberis*) is an excellent choice for a dense spiny hedge. Many have glossy leaves, similar to holly, and yellow or yellow-orange flowers in spring, followed by scarlet or purple berries in autumn and winter. This is a good choice if your soil is poor; barberries thrive in most areas.

If you want autumn colour and do not mind a deciduous hedge – the thorny stems will still provide a thick barrier – try a deciduous barberry such as *B. aggregata* 'Barbarossa'. This grows up to 1.8m/6ft, with pale to mid-green leaves that turn red and orange in autumn, and produces yellow flowers and scarlet berries.

By the sea

Escallonias love coastal areas, but are slightly tender and not recommended for very cold or exposed areas. Left to its own devices, *E. macrantha* will grow to 1.6-3m/6-10ft with a spread of 1.6m/6ft but can be trimmed to make a lower hedge. The glossy, deep green leaves are complemented by crimson flowers from summer

shrubs recommended, except the dwarf varieties, can easily be pruned to any height from 0.7-1.8m/2½-6ft.

A flowering hedge often has more to offer than simple flowers. Many also have bright berries or coloured stems or foto early autumn. Again, this needs pruning only once a year after flowering.

Old-fashioned touch

For the feel of a real country garden, *Rosa rugosa* is hard to beat. One of the older species roses, it is particularly resistant to pests and diseases. The prickly, hairy branches form an impenetrable thicket, and deep pink, heavily scented flowers appear from early summer to autumn, followed by round orange-red hips.

Alternatively, the floribunda 'Queen Elizabeth' rose carries striking pink flowers from early summer through to late autumn and, planted 30cm/1ft apart, forms a dense hedge.

If yellow is your colour, choose between cinquefoil (*Potentilla*) or forsythia. *Potentilla fruticosa* does well on even the poorest soil and is covered with beautiful lemon-yellow flowers from spring through to autumn.

Forsythia × *intermedia* 'Spectabilis' is ideal for early spring colour, with its golden-yellow flowers covering the branches. But it is suitable

Eric Crichton

Collections/Patrick Johns

PLANTS FOR DWARF FLOWERING HEDGES			
Name	**Description**	**Distance**	**Planting tips and maintenance**
Berberis thunbergii 'Atropurpurea Nana'	30-45cm/ 12-18in high, deciduous, purple-red leaves spring and summer, yellow flowers spring and summer, followed by scarlet berries.	30cm/12in	Plant autumn to spring, in sunny spot for best leaf colour. Trim after leaf fall.
Lavandula spica (syn. angustifolia) 'Hidcote' (lavender)	30-60cm/ 12-24in high, purple-blue flowers summer to autumn, silver-grey leaves	23-30cm/ 9-12in	Plant autumn to spring, in sunny spot. Clip into shape in spring. Renew after five or six years.
Santolina chamaecyparissus 'Nana' (cotton lavender)	30cm/12in high, evergreen, silvery leaves, bright yellow flowers in summer.	30cm/12in	Plant autumn or spring, in sunny spot. Pinch out growing points at intervals in first years. Trim in spring and dead-head after flowering.

Potentilla fruticosa (left), smothered with a profusion of buttercup-yellow flowers. Named varieties have other colours of blooms and flower between late spring and mid autumn. Keep potentilla bushy and vigorous by removing weak stems at ground level. It grows best in a sunny site on well-drained soil.

Osmanthus × burkwoodii (bottom) is a compact shrub that trims well into a neat hedge. The white flowers appear in mid and late spring. This hardy evergreen is a cross between O. decorus and O. delavayi.

Bridal wreath (Spiraea × vanhouttei) has cascading sprays of white flowers (right) in late spring and early summer.

Lavender (centre right) can make a very decorative dwarf hedge. Being neither child-proof nor stock-proof, it is best used within a garden, rather than as a boundary.

Brigitte Thomas/Garden Picture Library

Tania Midgley

only for a very informal hedge as it must be trimmed only lightly after flowering.

Keep it low

For lower flowering hedges to divide up the garden, it is hard to improve on lavender (*Lavandula*) or fuchsia, both planted about 20cm/8in apart. *Lavandula spica* 'Munstead' is a compact plant with silvery-green leaves that flowers profusely from early to late summer. One drawback is that the hedge will need replacing after five or six years.

The hybrid fuchsia 'Brilliant', with its large scarlet and magenta flowers, makes a striking, though seasonal, hedge some 60cm/2ft tall at most and should be cut down to ground level in the autumn.

You can always plant more than one type of flowering shrub in your hedge. A mixture can create a splendid backdrop to your lawn or herbaceous border and will ensure that your hedge is a focal point throughout the year.

WHAT WENT WRONG?

BRING BACK THE FLOWERS

Q Three years ago I inherited an established escallonia hedge. It was overgrown, so I have trimmed it back hard three times a year. Although it is neater, the flowers have been very disappointing. What should I do?

A Escallonia makes a wonderful informal hedge but, by cutting it back hard, you are destroying the wonderful flowers. For best results, trim your hedge only once a year, after flowering. You can then prune it back hard and the following year you should have long arching stems which cascade downwards, bearing excellent blooms.

Walls, Fences
and other Boundaries

The boundaries enclosing a garden are often regarded as a necessary evil, but a little thought can turn them into decorative assets, whether they are old or new.

Even if almost completely hidden by planting, the walls, fences or other garden boundaries are a very important part of the garden. Unless they are the minimal boundary markers found on open-plan housing estates, they occupy a lot of vertical space.

If you are planning to renew a boundary, give it plenty of thought, as it is a major decision, and one you will have to live with for many years. First, you must decide what is its major function – to provide privacy, keep out intruders and animals, act as a windbreak, screen off an ugly view or support plants. Usually an external boundary has to perform a mixture of all these.

Next, check which boundaries are yours, and which belong to your neighbours. This should be indicated in the title deeds to the house; if these are not available, as a rule you are responsible for those boundaries whose supports are on the side of your property.

How high?
The small size of modern gardens, and consequent closeness of neighbours, makes privacy an overriding need. This leads people to put up high fences – but these have a number of disadvantages. A high fence enclosing a small plot can make it look like a prison yard, especially when the fence is new and planting has yet to soften its outlines. Tall fences cast long shadows.

Harry Smith Collection

Derek Gould

Peter McHoy

In a small garden, shadows can stretch right across it for a considerable part of the day, plunging plants into growth-restricting gloom and encouraging moss in lawns. In windy areas, tall fences are at a further disadvantage as they are liable to be blown down.

Remember that in Britain there are legal restrictions about heights of boundaries. In the back garden, where your patch adjoins others, you can erect a fence up to 1.8m/6ft high without planning permission. In the front, or wherever your garden adjoins a highway, your limit is usually 1m/3ft. Some modern estates have special restrictions.

Generally speaking, it is best to go for the lowest fence that will do the job. A person of average height cannot see over a 1.5m/5ft high fence unless right up against it. You might consider, as a compromise, having a lower fence topped with trellis panels which will screen the view but let in light and reduce wind resistance.

Timber fencing

Wooden fences are the most popular type of garden boundary as they are quick and cheap to build compared with a wall, and provide instant results compared with a hedge, which may take years to grow.

Prefabricated panels have become an almost universal choice as they are so easy to put up – the 1.8m/6ft wide

The traditional closeboard fence (left), topped here with trellis, makes a most attractive, if expensive boundary.

A prefabricated lapped fence (top) is relatively cheap and easy to build.

If privacy is not a priority, open, diagonal panels (above) can provide an effective barrier.

Post spikes save having to dig a hole for the post. Some types can be tightened around the post (right).

Peter McHoy

POST HASTE

When replacing rotten fence posts, put the new ones into metal fence-post spikes. These are simply hammered into the ground, and the post slips into a square socket at the top. As well as avoiding messing about with concrete or rubble, the spike avoids future rotting as the post is not in the wet ground.

SHORT CUTS

89

panels are simply nailed to timber posts. No finishing is required, as they are pretreated against rot and insects.

There are two types: in one, the thin strips of larch wood making up the panel are overlapped, in the other they are interwoven. Lapped is best for privacy, as shrinkage in hot weather creates gaps in the interwoven type. Neither is very strong, and once damaged cannot be satisfactorily repaired.

Closeboard fencing, the traditional fence made from overlapping featheredge boards nailed to triangular cross rails (arris rails) is strong and completely peep-proof. Ideally, it should also have a capping strip to protect the top of the boards, and a gravel board at the bottom which can be removed and replaced when rotten. Such a fence is expensive, but can be tailored to any height and length, is long-lasting and easy to repair.

Interlap fencing is a very strong type of fence made by nailing square-edged boards to alternate sides of horizontal rails. The boards can be overlapped or butted together, for maximum privacy, or spaced apart for a decorative effect and to allow wind to pass through. Interlap fencing is not cheap, but it does look good on both sides.

Another traditional style is picket fencing, ideal for cottage-style gardens or front gardens where a strong barrier is desirable but privacy is not required. It is made from narrow vertical boards, either pointed or rounded at the top, nailed to cross rails about 5cm/2in apart and usually painted white. Prefabricated picket panels are available.

Utility fencing

Where appearance is not important, other conveniently prefabricated fencing can be used. Chain link fencing is made from rolls of galvanized or plastic-coated wire, woven into a diamond-shaped mesh. The mesh is fixed to heavy-duty wire stretched tightly between timber, concrete or angle iron posts. It is secure in that it keeps out animals and is difficult to climb, though the wire can be cut by a determined intruder. It can be hidden by a vigorous twining climber, or make an annual support for sweet peas. In time, it tends to sag as the supporting wires loosen.

Chestnut paling is sold in rolls of lightweight timber stakes, traditionally made of chestnut, set into loops of thick wire at the top and bot-

Photos Horticultural

S & O Matthews

tom to hold them upright between the posts. It lasts well, needs no maintenance and looks more attractive than chain link fencing, especially in a country setting.

A fence made from precast concrete horizontal sections slotted into concrete posts takes up as little width as a timber fence, but gives the security and privacy of a masonry wall. It is very ugly, but lasts many years and needs no maintenance of any kind.

Decorative markers

The example of modern open-plan estates has been followed in many front gardens by removing the old fences or hedges and installing low, mainly decorative barriers instead. In post and chain fencing, chunky square posts are linked by decorative chain links. Posts can be timber or plastic; the chain is usually metal or plastic.

Ranch fencing is a low but strong fence consisting of short posts linked by two or three tiers of horizontal boards. It is not purely decorative, and can keep animals

Peter McHoy

out. Plastic is often used instead of timber to eliminate maintenance.

Garden centres stock a variety of small prefabricated fence units mainly intended for defining interior spaces or edging flower beds. Popular designs include hooped plastic-coated wire resembling the type used to edge flower beds in public parks and white or black plastic patterns based

DON'T FORGET!

WIND LORE

As well as casting long shadows, solid high boundaries can cause wind turbulence in the garden. Unable to penetrate the barrier, the wind builds up, then tumbles over at greater velocity. The ideal wind barrier is one that allows air to filter through slowly.

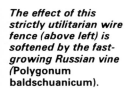

The effect of this strictly utilitarian wire fence (above left) is softened by the fast-growing Russian vine (Polygonum baldschuanicum).

Interwoven hurdles (left) provide traditional fencing in rural areas. Available from enterprising nurseries and garden centres, they are attractive, permeable and long-lasting.

Picket fencing (above right) is an ideal choice for a suburban front garden. An alternative is ranch fencing (right), here constructed of plastic, which can look good in front of many weatherboard houses and bungalows.

Peter McHoy

on traditional wrought-iron work designs.

Timber trellis made from cedar or softwood laths pinned together to form squares or diamonds cannot really form a fence on its own.

Trellis

Trellis has little structural strength, but it is extremely useful as an adjunct to other types of timber fencing, and for making interior partitions to support climbing plants.

The square type of trellis is rigid and strong – good for increasing the height of a panel fence – while diamond trellis can be pulled in and out like a concertina, enabling it to be fitted exactly to the space available. Cedar wood is the best material as it is slightly oily and needs no preservative treatment. Both types are available in a wide range of heights and widths.

Masonry walls

Nothing makes a better background for plants than a brick or stone wall. The cost is much higher than for fencing as, except for very low walls, building them is a job for a tradesman, but they offer complete security and privacy and are virtually indestructible.

If your house walls are brick, a brick boundary wall should be as close a match as possible. The same bricks may still be in production, even if the house was built some years ago; for an old house,

buy matching secondhand bricks. Low garden walls are sometimes made with only a single thickness of brick, but these look rather flimsy and are prone to cracking. The traditional double skin wall is stronger and better-looking. Brick screen walls, with gaps between the bricks, should be built with piers for added strength. Such walls can make decorative features, especially when combined with a brick barbecue or arch.

Real stone is prohibitively expensive, but many reconstituted stone blocks are good imitations. A stone wall should look as if it is made from locally quarried stone – scout round the neighbourhood to see what old stone walls are like. Man-made stones are available in a wide variety of styles, finished to resemble semi-dressed natural stone blocks – uniform in shape but with one rough-hewn face.

Plain concrete blocks are strictly utilitarian, but pierced decorative blocks can be quite attractive in the right setting. They are often used to make screen walls across a garden, concealing but still revealing what lies beyond. Screen walling is most effective when the house has a rendered finish and both the wall and house can be painted the same colour.

If your existing boundaries are not what you would have chosen, do not despair – there is a lot you can do to turn them

A trellis with climbers (above) makes an attractive if lightweight boundary.

Pieris and ivies (above right) mask the uniform pattern of man-made stone.

Ceanothus (above far right) can enhance a stone wall. This variety is 'Puget Blue'.

Pierced concrete blocks (right) add a decorative feature to a low brick wall.

into assets, not eyesores.

First attend to any essential repairs – a slightly dilapidated look has a certain charm, but a leaning fence or bulging wall will eventually collapse. The silver-grey colour of weathered timber makes a good background for climbing plants, but if you want a rather smarter look, paint the fence with timber preservative.

If you have modern windows with a timber finish, paint the fence a matching colour for a very smart look. Avoid gloss paint, which deteriorates quickly. Where a fence already has a paint finish, sand it down and repaint with a water-based MVP (moisture vapour permeable) paint. These are easy to apply and last better, as they are elastic and allow water vapour that settles to escape.

Repointing a wall will automatically smarten it up.

Brick is best left unpainted, but if this has already been done, repaint with masonry paint which lasts for years.

A coat of masonry paint can transform an ugly concrete block wall – white is usually the most successful. If you have the type of wall with a hollow top, try growing tumbling alpine plants, or add a new, flat coping and decorate it with potted plants for a smart Mediterranean look.

Plants to the rescue

Plants are the best way to turn your boundaries into assets. A south- or west-facing masonry wall retains warmth and is invaluable as a backing for slightly tender shrubs like Californian lilac (*Ceanothus*). Even cold north or east-facing boundaries can be clothed with suitable plants.

Regard any wall or fence as a support for a climbing plant

– but don't forget that, once flourishing, it will add considerable extra weight to the structure. If you want permanent cover for an eyesore, choose evergreen clinging or twining plants such as ivies. Use evergreen shrubs to break up the outline of a long stretch of high fence or wall, or build in a crossways trellis planted with climbing roses.

A fence shared with a friendly neighbour can be made attractive on both sides with plants such as clematis and honeysuckle, which will scramble up one side, then tumble down the other, to the benefit of both parties. If a complete barrier is not required you could even plant a screen of bamboo or evergreen shrubs instead of a fence.

BRIGHT IDEAS

MINI HEDGE

If you would really like a hedge but only have room for a fence, turn it into a fedge. Plant ivy at intervals of about 1m/3ft. Once it is established it will soon clothe the bare wood with rich green.

Index

Page numbers in *italic* refer to illustrations

A

Abutilon x *suntense 43*, 44
    A. megapotamicum 25
Acer palmatum 45
    'Dissectum Atropurpureum'
      46
Alyssum saxatile 47
annuals 13, 37
    climbers 9-11, 19, 25, 33, 35,
      77
apple 21, *63, 64*, 65
    'James Grieve' *64*
arabis 47
arbours 11, 12-16, 22
    climbers for 13
arches 6-11, 30, 43
    plants for 10
armeria 50
Aronia arbutifolia 45
Artemisia arborescens 16
Arundinaria 20
    A. murielae 18
aubrietia 47, 48
aucuba 20, 35
    A. japonica 'Variegata' *18*
autumn 33, 45, 46
azalea *34*

B

bamboo 18, 20, *32*, 35, 93
banks *36*, 39-40, 53
barberry 20, 80, 85
baskets: hanging *7, 9*, 33, *33*,
    71-3
    wall 47
beans 11, 74, 75, *76, 77*, 78
beech 18, 80, *80*, 83
begonia 37
Berberis 35, 45, *80*, 81, 85
    B. aggregata 'Barbarossa' 85
    B. darwinii 44
    B. x *stenophylla* 44, 80, *84*, 85
    B. thunbergii 'Atropurpurea
      Nana' 86
berries 20, 34, 45
Betula pendula 18
birch 17-18
birds 66-7, 70, 80, 83
black-eyed Susan 11, 25
borders 46, 53
boundaries *21*, 22, 84, 88-93
bowers 13
box 80, 81, 82
brickwork *6, 9*, 15
bridal wreath 38, *87*
Buxus sempervirens 82

C

Calendula officinalis 82
Californian lilac 44, 93
Calluna vulgaris 45
camellia 46
    C. x *williamsii* 45, *45*
Campanula carpatica 47
    C. portenschlagiana 50
Campsis 77*, 92*
    C. radicans 42*, 42*
Canary creeper 19, 25, 33
Carpinus betula 18
Caryopteris x *clandonensis* 45
cathedral bells 11
catkins 34
Ceanothus 44*, 93*
    C. impressus (Santa Barbara)
      25
    'Puget Blue' *93*
cedar, western red 13
Chaenomeles 44
    C. speciosa 50
      'Phyllis Moore' *44*
    C. x *superba* 34
Chamaecyparis lawsoniana
    'Lanei' 21
cherry, flowering 32
    'Morello' *67*
    'Stella', fan-trained *65*
Chilean glory flower 11, 77
Chilean potato tree *22, 24*
Chinese lantern 25
chives 82
Choisya ternata 46, 80, 82
chokeberry, red 45
cinquefoil 45, 86
Cistus 44
clematis *6, 9*, 18, 23, 25, 32,
    35, 40, 43, 50, 52-7, *75*,
    77, 78, 80
    C. alpina (alpine c.) 28, 37,
      52, 53, 54
    C. armandii 'Apple
      Blossom' 33, 40
    'Beauty of Worcester' 28
    'Bees Jubilee' 77
      'Frances Rivis' 40, 54, *55*
    C. chrysocoma 44
    C. cirrhosa balearica 33
    'Crimson King' 54
    'Ernest Markham' 28
    C. flammula 38
    C. florida 'Sieboldii' 56, *56*
    for arbours 13
    for arches & pergolas 10
    for containers 36-7
    for entrances 26-7, 28
    for ground cover 38
    'Gipsy Queen' 77
    'Hagley Hybrid' *30*
    'Henryi' 55
    C. integrifolia 53, *53*
    C. x *jackmanii* 52-3, 56
      'Superba' 28, *29*, 56
    C. x *jouiniana* 'Cote d'Azur'
      38
    'Lady Betty Balfour' 77
    'Lasurstern' 28, *62*, 77
    C. macropetala (Chinese c.)
      33, 37, 52, 53, *55*
      'Maidwell Hall' *37*
      'Markham's Pink' 37, 54
    'Miss Bateman'*33*
    C. montana (mountain c.) 28,
      28, 35, 40, 41, 52, 53, *53*
      'Elizabeth' 21, 51, 54
      rubens 10, *41*
      'Tetrarose' *18*, 54
    'Nelly Moser' 27, 28, *29, 52*,
      54
    C. orientalis (orange-peel
      clematis) 13, 37, 53, 54, *55*
      'Vyvyan Pennell' 54, *55*
    'Perle d'Azur' *29*
    'Proteus' 54, *56*
    C. recta 53
    'Rouge Cardinale' 55, *56*
    C. tangutica 28, 37, 38, 43,
      53, *53*
    'Ville de Lyon' 28, *29, 62*
    C. viticella 13, 39, 43, 46, 53
      'Abundance' *14*
      'Purpurea Plena Elegans'
        56
    'Vyvyan Pennell' 28
    'Yellow Queen' *76*
climbers 33, 42-3
    annual 9-11, 19, 25, 33, 35,
      77
    buying 27-8
    as creepers 36-41
    for arbours 13
    for arches & pergolas 10, 18
    for entrances 26-30
    for walls 50
    perennial 25, 77
    planting 10-11, 25, 29, 43
Cobaea scandens 11, 33, 77
colonnades 43
compost heap, screening 34
concreting uprights 7-9, 15
conifers 13, *21*, 31, 47, *79*
containers 19, 20, *22, 23*, 25,
    30, 33, 34, *34*, 36-8, 46
    ivies 70, 71-3
    wall 47, 90
    wigwams in 74, *75*, 78
cordons 63, 64-6, *64, 65, 67*, 82
Cornus 85
    C. alba 46
      'Spaethii' *40*

Corylus avellana 'Contorta' 46
Cotinus coggygria 21, 44, 45
    'Foliis Purpureis' *44*, 46
    'Royal Purple' 46
cotoneaster 20, 45, *48*
    'Cornubia' 46, 80
    C. horizontalis 34, 37, *37*,
      38
    C. simonsii 46
    C. x *watereri* 'Cornubia' *46*
cottage-style garden 6, *8*, 30
cotton lavender 80, 82, 86
crab apple 18
creepers 36-41
creosote 15
crocus 48
cup & saucer plant 11, 33, 77
x *Cupressocyparis leylandii*
    (Leyland cypress) 17, 19, 80,
    81, 83

D

daphne 32
deciduous shrubs 44, 45-6
deutzia 46
dianthus *50*
    D. alpinus 48
dogwood *40*, 46, 85
drainpipes, disguising 32-4
dry-stone walls *47, 48*
dustbin, screening 34-5

E

Eccremocarpus scaber 11, 18,
    77
Elaeagnus pungens 'Maculata'
    18, 44, 46
entrances 26-30, *43*
Erica x *darleyensis* 45
Escallonia 21, 44, *84*, 85, 87
    E. macrantha 80, 85
espaliers 63, *64*, 65-6, *65*
Euonymus europaeus 'Red
    Cascade' 45
    E. fortunei 34, 46, 50
evergreens 13, 18-20, 33, *35*,
    44, 80

F

Fagus sylvatica 18, 80
fan fruit trees *63, 64*, 66-7
fan trellis 23, *23, 24*
Fatsia japonica 46
fences *19*, 32, 40-1, 88-92
firethorn 44, 80, 85
flannel bush 25
flower-arranging 46
flowering shrubs 44-5

foliage shrubs 45-6
forsythia 38, 44, 46, *83*, 86
   F. x *intermedia* 'Spectabilis'
     80, 86
foxglove 46
fragrance *8*, 11, 13, *16*, 21, 32
fremontia 25
Fremontodendron californicum
   25, *43*, 44
front door *see* entrance
fruit trees, wall-trained 63-7
fuchsia 45, 87

G

garage, screening *21, 32*
Garrya elliptica 34, 50
geranium *8*, *49*
grape hyacinth 46, *48*
Griselinia littoralis 21, 80
ground cover *37*, 38, *38*, 40,
   40, 53, 70-2, *70*
guttering, disguising 32-4

H

Hamamelis x *intermedia* 44
hawthorn 80
hazel 80
   corkscrew 46
heather 45, 46, 48
Hebe 44, 45, 82
Hedera 13, 42, 92
   H. azorica 'Typica' 70
   H. canariensis 'Azorica' 39
     'Gloire de Marengo' 38, 70
     'Variegata' *68*
   H. colchica 39, *68*, 70
     'Dentata Variegata' *36*,
      38, 70
     'Sulphur Heart' 70, *70*
   H. helix 32, 38, *38*, 69
     'Adam' 70, 73
     'Anne Marie' 71
     'Atropurpurea' 33, 73
     'Brokamp' 70, 71
     'Buttercup' 39, *68*, 70,
      71, *71*
     'Chester' 71
     'Deltoidea' 70, 71, *71*
     'Dragon Claw' 71
     'Erecta' 73
     'Fluffy Ruffles' 73
     'Glacier' 33, 70, *70*, 71
     'Glymii' 70, 73
     'Goldheart' 9, 10, *10*, 18,
      33, *38*, 49, *69*, 70, 71
     'Jubilee' 49
     'Kolibri' 70, 73, *73*
     'Manda's Crested' 49,
      73, *73*
     'Midas Touch' 70, 73
     'Poetica' *69*, 70, 73
     'Succinata' 73
hedges 20, 59, *60*, 61, 63, 79-83
   arbour 13, 14-15
   brightening 41
   dwarf 86, 87

edible 82
   flowering 84-7
   plants 80
   prickly 81, 85-6
   screens 18, *19, 34*
helianthemum 48
Helleborus orientalis 46
herbs 51, 82
holly 46, 80, 81
   hedgehog 81
honeysuckle *6*, *8*, 11, *12*, 13,
   16, 21, 25, 32, *32*, 33, *37*, 40,
   41, 43, 46, 49, 58-62, 80
   box *60*
   Dutch 60
   evergreen 13
   Japanese 25, 37, *59*
hop 80
   golden 9, 10, *10*
hornbeam 14, 18, 80
houseleek 50
houseplants 70
Humulus lupulus 50
   'Aureus' 9, 10, *10*
hydrangea *46*
   H. petiolaris (climbing h.) 9,
     10, 33, 39, 42, 50, 92

I

Ilex aquifolium 80
   'Ferox Argentea' 81
insects 62, 70, 80
Ipomoea 9-11
   I. tricolor 'Heavenly Blue' *77*
iris 46
ivy *8*, 9, 13, 18, *31*, 32, 33, 35,
   36, *36*, 38, *38*, 42, 47, *48*, 49
   68-73, 77, 92, 93, *93*
   Canary Island 9, 38, 39
   candelabra 73
   English 9, 10
   Persian *36*, 38, 39, 70
   poet's 73
   sweetheart 71

J

Jasminum (jasmine) 11, 13, 32,
   33, 43
   J. nudiflorum (winter) 10,
     25, 33, 35, 51
   J. officinale (summer) 13,
     21, *24*, 35
   J. polyanthum 25
   star *15*
juniper *83*

K

kissing bough 69
knot garden 81-2

L

larch poles 43
Lathyrus odoratus 11, 25, 33, 77
laurel 80

laurustinus 45
Lavandula (lavender) 21, *48*,
   81, 82, 87, *87*
   L. spica 'Hidcote' *83*, 86
     'Munstead' 87
lenten rose 46
lettuce 82
Lewisia cotyledon howellii 50
Ligustrum ovalifolium 46, 80
   'Aureo Marginatum' *81*
ling 45
lobelia 37, 47
long narrow garden 19
Lonicera 13, 58-62
   'Early Dutch' *61*
   L. x *americana* 8, 11, *12*, 49,
     58-9, 60
   L. x *brownii* 24, *59*, 61
   L. fragrantissima 46
   L. henryi 61
   L. japonica 46
     'Aureoreticulata' 25, 33,
      37, *37*, 46, 61, *61*
     'Halliana' *59*
   L. nitida 13, *59*, 61
     'Baggesen's Gold' 18,
      60, 61
   L. periclymenum 25, 60-1
     'Belgica' 25, *59*, 60
     'Serotina' 25, 60
   L. pileata 46
   L. syringantha 61
   L. x *tellmanniana* 62
   L. tragophylla 61

M

Magnolia delavayi 34
   M. grandiflora 34
   M. stellata 8
mahonia 81
   M. japonica 45, *45*, 46
Malus floribunda 18
Mandevilla 13
manhole covers 34, *34*
maple, Japanese 45, 46
marigold, French *77*
   pot 82
mesh netting 23, 24, 29
metal: constructions *8, 16*
   stake supports 7-9, 15
Mexican orange blossom 80, 82
mignonette 13
mock orange, golden 46
morning glory 9-11
moss 49-50, *51*

N

Nandina domestica 35
nasturtium 11, *31*, 33, 37, 76,
   77, *77*
Nicotiana 13
   N. sylvestris 21

O

Osmanthus x *burkwoodii* 87

P

pansy 47
parterre 82
Parthenocissus henryana 33,
   48-9
   P. quinquefolia 33, 42, *42*
Passiflora caerulea 10, 13, 21,
   25, 50, 77
patio screens 18, *19*, 20-1, 82
peach, fan-trained *67*
pear *65*
pelargonium 19, *31*
perennial climbers 25, 77
pergolas 6-11, 15, 21, *32, 43*,
   51
   plants for 10, 18
periwinkle, greater 38
pest control 60
Philadelphus coronarius
   'Aureus' 46
pieris *93*
pinks 51
pipes, disguising 32-*4*
Pittosporum tenuifolium 46
planting boxes 47
polyanthus *51*
Polygonum baldschuanicum
   14, 18, 40, 50, 91
porch 27
post spikes 51, *89*
Potentilla 45, 86
   P. arbuscula 80
   P. fruticosa 86, *86*
potholders *31*, 33
privet 80, 81, *81*
   oval-leaved 13, 46
Prunus 'Amanogawa' 32
   P. subhirtella 'Autumnalis' 32
Pyracantha 20, 34, 44, *81*
   P. rogersiana 80, 85

Q

quince 34, 44, 50

R

rhododendron 46
   dwarf 48
Rhus typhina 46
Robinia pseudoacacia 'Frisia'
   18
rock rose 48
rockery 48
Rosa (rose) *6*, 9, 18, 20, 22, 28,
   41
   'Bantry Bay' *71*
   climbing 11, 13, 25, *26*, 27-8,
     30, 32, 35, 43, *49*, 77, 93
     'Aloha' 28, 39
     'Cécil Brunner' 41
     'Danse du Feu' 28, *30*
     'Etoile de Hollande' *27*, 28
     'François Juranville' 41
     'Galway Bay' 22
     'Golden Showers' 28, 29,
      33, 51

'Handel' 28, *29*
'Juno' 39
'La Ville de Bruxelles' 39
'Mermaid' 28
'Mme Alfred Carrière' 28, *30*
'Mme Grégoire Staechelin' 11, *11*
'New Dawn' 33
'Pompon de Paris' *24*, 25
'Schoolgirl' 28
'Swan Lake' 28
'Zéphirine Drouhin' 28
R. ecae 'Helen Knight' 25
floribunda 86
ground-sprawling 40
'Scintillation' 40, *40*
hedges 81
R. paulii rosea 40
pillar *30*, 32
rambling 11, 13, 25, 27, 32, 43, 77
'Iceberg' *12*
R. rugosa *83*, 85, *85*, 86
'Frau Dagmar Hastrup' 81
shrub 45, *57*
suckers 29
rosemary 81, 82
rustic poles *6*, *7*, *8*, 11, 13

S

Santolina chamaecyparissus 80, 82
'Nana' 86
sawn timber 7-9, *9*
saxifrage 48, 50
screens 17-21, 22, 31-5, 74, 84
plants for 18
seating 16
sedum 50

S. acre 48
self-clinging climbers 32, 42, 92
semi-evergreens 46
sempervivum 50
S. gamma *51*
senecio *48*
S. greyi *81*
shade, climbers for 25, 28, 33
shed, screening *32*
shrubs 42-6
flowering hedges 85
planting 44
wall 25, 43-4
Skimmia japonica 80
sloe 80
smoke tree 21, 44, *44*, 45
purple 46
snowdrop 46
soft fruit 21
Solanum crispum 22
Sorbus aria 'Lutescens' 18-19
S. vilmorinii 18
specimen planting 21, 46
spindle 45
spiraea 45
S. x arguta 38
S. thunbergii 85
S. x vanhouttei 87
spring-flowering shrubs 45, 46
statues *37*, 38
steps, garden 38
stocks 13
stonecrop 48
sumach, stag's horn 46
summer-flowering shrubs 45
sun rose 44
supports 29-30, 42-3, 57
see also trellis
sweet pea 11, 19, 25, 33, *75*, 76, 77

T

thrift *50*
Thuja plicata 13
Thunbergia alata 11, 25
thyme 51, 82
ties 30
tobacco plant 21
tomato plants 48
topiary *35*, 71, *79*, 81, 82
Trachelospermum jasminoides 13, *15*
trailing plants 36-41, 47
tree stumps 39
trees: arbours 13-14
growing climbers over 41, *41*, 43, 52, 57
screens 17-19, 21, 31-2
trellis 22-5, *29*, 32, 33, 42, 51, 57, *92*, 92
arbour *12*, 13, *14*, 15
arch *8*
column *24*
fixing 24, 51
making your own 20
screens *17*, *18*, *19*, 20
tripods 43
Tropaeolum 11, 33, 77
T. majus 33
T. peregrinum 11, 19, 25, 33, 77
T. speciosum 11
troughs 37-8, 48
trumpet vine 42, *42*, 77, 92
tubs 36-7
twiners 43

V

vegetable plot, screening *34*
veronica, shrubby 44, 45
Viburnum tinus 45

Vinca major 'Variegata' 38
vine 13, 33, 35
crimson glory 33, *39*, 41
grape 21, 43, 51
hop *10*, 50
mile-a-minute 40
Russian *14*, 18, 50, *91*
vine eyes 30, 32
viola *50*
Virginia creeper 33, 42, *42*, 92
Vitis 33
'Brant' 33, 43
V. coignetiae 33, *39*, 41
V. quinquefolia 92

W

wall shrubs 25, 32, 34, 43-4, 50
wallflower 50
walls *31*, 32, 40, 70-1, 92-3
low *37*, 38, 47-51
plants grown in 50-1, *50-1*
rain shadow 48
stone-facing 49
wall-trained fruit trees 63-7
water butt, screening *33*, *35*
wigwams 74-8
windbreaks *19*, 21, 82-3, 91
window boxes 37, 73
winter flowers 33, 45, 46, 85
wire supports 30, 32, 43, *63*
wisteria 9, *10*, 21, 32, 43
W. floribunda 'Macrobotrys' (Japanese) 10, 13, *13*, 21
witch hazel 44
wood preservative 7, 15
woodbine *59*, 60-1
Chinese *61*

Y

yew 13, 39, 80, 81
yucca 46

*P*HOTOGRAPHIC *C*REDITS

ANDREW LAWSON *12, 14, 15, 20, 33, 58, 61, 62, 74, 80, 92*
BOYS SYNDICATION *30*; COLLECTIONS *51, 86*
DAVID SQUIRE *13, 20, 24, 25, 37, 41, 50*
DEREK GOULD *7, 23, 51, 83, 89, 93*; DON WILDRIDGE *18, 81*
ERIC CRICHTON *6, 9, 14, 25, 32, 44, 50, 52, 53, 59, 60, 61, 63, 65, 68, 71, 76, 82, 83, 86, 92*
EWA *27, 30*; GARDEN PICTURE LIBRARY *17, 18, 19, 31, 40, 42, 46, 47, 48, 69, 77, 79, 87*
GILLIAN BECKET *32, 34, 43, 69, 71*
HARRY SMITH COLLECTION *8, 16, 24, 25, 29, 30, 37, 53, 55, 56, 58, 60, 61, 64, 67, 71, 75, 88, 93*
JOHN GLOVER *62*; KENNETH SCOWEN *29*; MARSHALL CAVENDISH *10, 11, 29, 78*
NEIL HOLMES *6, 23, 26, 33, 65*; PAT BRINDLEY *10, 19, 27, 28, 29, 73, 76*
PETER McHOY *36, 45, 48, 49, 59, 73, 80, 81, 89, 91*
PHOTOS HORTICULTURAL *12, 14, 15, 20, 22, 29, 34, 35, 38, 40, 42, 46, 49, 53, 54, 55, 56, 57, 59, 65, 66, 70, 84, 85, 90*
S & O MATHEWS *16, 45, 90*; TANIA MIDGLEY *8, 35, 37, 38, 39, 41, 43, 45, 65, 76, 82, 87*